That's Just The Way It Is

*A realistic view of life
from the Book of Ecclesiastes*

Derek Tidball

Christian Focus

© Derek Tidball

ISBN 1 85792 331 6

Scripture quotations, unless otherwise indicated, are from
The New International Version,
© 1973, 1978, 1984 by the International Bible Society.

This edition published in 1998 by Christian Focus Publications,
Geanies House, Fearn, Ross-shire, IV20 1TW, Great Britain.
Previously published in 1989 as *That's Life*.

Cover design by Donna Macleod

Contents

PREFACE

Francis Schaeffer once wrote, 'There is a time, and ours is such a time, when a negative message is needed before anything positive can begin.... People often say to me, "What would you do if you met a really modern man on a train and you had just an hour to talk to him about the gospel?" I would spend forty-five minutes on the negative, to show him his real dilemma – to show him that he is more dead than even he thinks he is.... Then I would take ten or fifteen minutes to tell him the gospel.... Unless he understands what is wrong, he will not be ready to listen to, and understand, the positive.'[1]

The author of Ecclesiastes would have applauded Schaeffer's approach, assuming, that is, that he adopts his negative perspective as a technique rather than as a genuine expression of his own despair. Either way, the Preacher, as we shall call the author, drags us through the pointlessness and stupidity of life, often with great humour. Only very occasionally does he give us a glimpse of light. But in writing as he does, he sets down what we all feel and touches many of our raw nerves. It is a book which speaks for and to our generation, as it has often done before.

I have sought to write a light, contemporary exposition of Ecclesiastes. I am well aware that there are several points where other interpretations of the enigmatic Preacher's meaning is possible. I am also aware of much debate on who the Preacher was and other matters of introduction. I would encourage the reader who wants to dig deeper into some of these issues to consult the commentaries on these matters.

I have not regarded it as my task, as a preacher, to go into these matters in depth. My task has been to let the book speak clearly and to apply it to our times. This does not mean that I have ignored these questions or alternative interpretations. It

5

means that, coming to the book as a preacher, I have weighed them and then decided, rightly or wrongly, my conclusion and put it before my congregation. Most congregations want to see the wood for the trees and I do not think it should usually be part of a preacher's job to confuse them by offering half a dozen different interpretations of a text and leave them to choose. That is the task of the teacher in the classroom, and only occasionally of the preacher in the pulpit. The preacher needs to be aware of the interpretations and then, having, judiciously and prayerfully made up his own mind, put a clear word from the Lord before his people.

I have tried to keep references to a minimum so that they do not interrupt the flow of the addresses. My debts will be evident in those notes. It might also be said that in committing the spoken word to written form it was illuminating to discover how much material we preachers use which is not carefully footnoted. Sources were carefully checked at the time, but it has sometimes proved difficult to recover their details subsequently.

The addresses were originally given to my congregation at Mutley Baptist Church, Plymouth, in the summer of 1986. I would like to express my appreciation to them for their response to the messages and for their encouragement. I have long felt an attraction to this book as one which matches our times. I offer the expositions now as a humble attempt to unlock a book which is closed to many and to breathe life into it so that we may hear its invitation to remember our Creator.

Derek J Tidball

References
1. Francis Schaeffer, *Death in the City* (IVP, 1969) pp. 68ff.

1

LIFE'S LIKE THAT
1: 1-11

The words of the Teacher, son of David, king of Jerusalem:
^{2}"Meaningless! Meaningless!"
    says the Teacher.
"Utterly meaningless!
    Everything is meaningless."
^{3}What does man gain from all his labour
    at which he toils under the sun?
^{4}Generations come and generations go,
    but the earth remains for ever.
^{5}The sun rises and the sun sets,
    and hurries back to where it rises.
^{6}The wind blows to the south
    and turns to the north;
round and round it goes,
    ever returning on its course.
^{7}All streams flow into the sea,
    yet the sea is never full.
To the place the streams come from,
    there they return again.
^{8}All things are wearisome,
    more than one can say.
The eye never has enough of seeing,
    nor the ear its fill of hearing.
^{9}What has been will be again,
    what has been done will be done again;
    there is nothing new under the sun.
^{10}Is there anything of which one can say,
    "Look! This is something new"?
It was here already, long ago;
    it was here before our time.
^{11}There is no remembrance of men of old,
    and even those who are yet to come

7

will not be remembered
  by those who follow.

The story is told of the guest who approached his hostess at a party. 'I find the whole situation absurd, no-one seems to realise the silliness, the grotesque artificiality of their behaviour.'

'Ah,' said the hostess, 'you must join the sociologist in the far corner. The rest of us realised all that long ago but decided to ignore it and enjoy the party.'[1]

Ecclesiastes was written by a man who decided not to ignore reality any longer but to join the deviants in the corner who were honestly confronting the absurdity of life. And he invites us to join the conversation.

Few are comfortable with such honesty. A long hard look at everyday life can be very disconcerting. T.S. Eliot rightly warned that 'humankind cannot bear very much reality'. As our fantasies are unmasked and our rose-tinted spectacles are removed we are liable to slide into pessimism and to experience pain. But the author of Ecclesiastes will not let us escape back to our make-believe world too easily.

In spite of the fact the author introduces himself (*verse 1*), we do not know who he is. He describes himself as 'the Teacher, son of David, king of Jerusalem'. Some have thought that such clues point to the conclusion that Solomon wrote the book. But for a number of reasons it is unlikely that he was its author. Its language, references back to Solomon's time, and radical conclusions would suggest otherwise.

The anonymous author, whom contemporary language might speak of as 'Mr Preacher', does however have two legitimate reasons for linking himself with Solomon. First, he might be paraphrasing the experience of King Solomon, the wealthiest, wisest and most prestigious man who ever lived. He is writing about the things that Solomon struggled with. Solomon tried everything but was satisfied with nothing;

investigated everything but discovered at the end that he found nothing; owned everything and yet realised he possessed nothing; and had been into everything and yet was still left profoundly empty.

Secondly, the author stands in the tradition of Solomon as a writer of wisdom literature. Such literature was thoroughly down-to-earth. It dealt with mundane everyday matters and shunned high-flying theological answers. It provided rational examinations of life and, if read too quickly, almost seemed to leave God out. What Mr Preacher was doing had been done before, except that none had taken it as far as he did. He is the most radical in his tradition, questioning everything and leaving no sacred stone unturned. It is easy to see why some regard him as sceptical and as providing no answers to the puzzle that life is. Jeremiah and Job had both voiced the agony of the same perplexities and yet their faith shone through their doubts triumphantly. With Mr Preacher you are less sure. His scepticism matches the mood of our own day. He's exactly where many are at.

Whether his scepticism is real or merely a device to get us thinking is hotly debated. But even if you conclude that it is a device, it is not 'merely' a device. He deeply feels the questions he raises. He is not concerned to erect straw men simply so that he can quickly demolish them and introduce the truth. He is not engaged in a slight of hand, producing God, as a magician produces a rabbit from a hat, while you are mesmerised by the world. He is genuinely caught up in the questions and enigmas of life. Not for nothing has he been called 'the joker in the Old Testament pack'.[2]

Mr Preacher also introduces his conclusion (*verse 2*). It is a bit like a detective novel where the writer puts the last page first. You find out who did it and then you read the story so that you can see the clues being pieced together.

His conclusion is that life is 'Meaningless! Meaningless! Utterly meaningless! Everything is meaningless.'

He is not prejudging the issue. It is not like a poor piece of postgraduate research where you fix the conclusions you want to reach before you start and then look around for the evidence that fits while carefully ignoring bits which may be inconvenient. Nor is he trying to pressurise us into agreeing with him before we have had time to make up our own minds.

His approach is simply a typical Jewish way of writing. He says the most important thing first – so you don't miss it – and then goes on to justify it.

The phrase 'Meaningless! Meaningless! Utterly meaningless!' comes up thirty times in the book one way or another. He is saying that life, when you look at it hard enough, is 'a wisp or vapour, a puff of wind, a mere breath – nothing you can get your hands on; the nearest thing to zero'.[3] Life is empty, useless, insignificant, zilch! Life is brief and insubstantial. It is also cruel and deceptive for it promises much and fails to live up to its promise; offers much but delivers little.

Having stated his conclusion, Mr Preacher now sets about proving it and in the opening chapter presents a bird's-eye view of his case. He sets out six claims about life.

Life is boring (1:3)
'What does a man gain from all his labour at which he toils under the sun?' Life is a grind. It is so plain boring. What does anyone get out of it, considering all the hard slog to which they seem to be sentenced?

The basic problem for most people is not that life is a great tragedy. It isn't! In fact, sometimes a tragedy is welcomed as an interruption, as something different from the routine, something to get excited about, even if the emotions and consequences involved are negative. But most people go through life without great tragedies.

The basic problem is that life is composed of pointless drudgery. It is like living in a prison. Day in and day out there is the same routine. When the bell goes, or the warders knock on the cell door, the inmate has to get up and slop out. After the washing, he queues for breakfast. But to what point? There is nothing to do afterwards. Maybe there are a few chores; working in the laundry room or a few hours in the workshop. But the routine goes on its tyrannical course and all to no purpose. At the end of the day, or sooner if the officers are in short supply, they lock the prisoners back in their cells only for the same routine to be repeated tomorrow. It goes on relentlessly for a year, two years, five years or ten – whatever the judge has decided. The same old routine. But what has anyone to show for it? The prisoner is not going to grow or develop or achieve. It's just a monotonous boring repetition.

Many people live in open prisons. They live their lives at the dictates of routines and habits. But to what end? A hippie described his father's life like this:

> People becoming automated. Take my father. Get up, 7.30 breakfast, out at 8; get the 8.30 train to Charing Cross, get on the tube, off at Oxford Circus, walk along to Hanover Square. He goes upstairs, he sits there all day; he goes out for lunch – gets himself a beer and sandwich, comes back, carries on work, 5.30 he packs in, gets the tube back to Charing Cross, train home. I mean what a life! Where does it get you?[4]

Just think of it! The petty routines act as our prison warders! Up, wash, shave, clean teeth, breakfast, kick the cat, kiss the wife and off to catch the train to work. On returning home, read the newspaper, put the dustbin out, engage in DIY, lie exhausted in front of the TV. Or, it's Monday so it must be washing day; it's Tuesday so it must be shopping; it's

Wednesday so it must be coffee morning: it's Thursday so it must be more shopping – and so on. It's everyday so it must be cooking, cooking and more cooking. And what's the point?

Most of us welcome any break from the prison routine. A royal occasion comes and we hope to have a day off and watch it on the television. At least it will be a different day. A blizzard arrives and we can't make it into work. A national tragedy occurs and we have a welcome distraction. The boredom is punctured. Even Bank Holidays are welcome, provided they do not come too often or else they might just become part of the boring routine.

Routines are not all bad. We may wish it were not so but most of us need them to get through. Life would be unbearable without them. We could not cope with the unstructured freedom which would surround us. How thankful we should be that we do not have to decide from scratch every day whether we should clean our teeth or go to work or not. If existing routines were absent we would soon invent new ones for our own protection. But we take to them as if we were premature residents in an old people's home. We up and dress and sit staring into space in the lounge until bedtime with no real sense of purpose at all.

Not even work provides much fulfilment. We might argue from a theological point of view, as some do, and try to prove that it should be a deeply satisfying experience which imitates the fantastic creativity of God. But the experience of most people is different. For them it is just a question of clocking on, then watching the clock all day, until they can clock off. Getting out as soon as they can; inventing mental games and exercises for sheer survival; enjoying the distraction of talking about *United's* latest defeat or last night's *Coronation Street*; getting away with doing as little as possible; anything to dull the pain of the sheer boredom: that's what work is, for most people.

Clive Jenkins and Barrie Sherman of the Scientific, Technical and Managerial Staffs Association have admitted as much:

> By and large people neither enjoy their work, nor do they enjoy travelling to and from it. Most jobs are repetitive, require little if any personal initiative and, for the most part, people are incapable of fulfilling anything like their full potential through them.... People go to work that they do not enjoy, and spend a considerable proportion of their working hours getting to work and then home. It thus looms large in a life that is not very pleasant at the outset.[5]

Leisure is no real alternative. The increasing amount of leisure time available through changes in the pattern of work only serves to increase boredom. *The Times* carried a Reuters report from Peking on 8 April, 1986 saying 'Rich Chinese peasants are turning to crime, especially rape, to beat boredom spawned of leisure, according to an official newspaper, the *Tanjin Daily News.*'

The same boredom quickly descends on even the most exciting advances of mankind. In 1969 we were wide-eyed with wonder when Neil Armstrong walked on the moon. It was 'a small step for man, one giant leap for mankind'. We had introduced a new age. It was going to be tremendous. But by 1980 Dr Lewis Thomas wrote in *Harvard Magazine*: 'You can walk on the moon if you like, but there's nothing to do there except look at the earth; and when you've seen one earth, you've seen them all.'[6] Even the most exciting novelties quickly become boring.

Life is fragile (1:4)
Every baby should be delivered, gift-wrapped, with the label 'Fragile – right side up' firmly attached! As if Mr Preacher is not already pessimistic enough he finds another reason to engage in the power of negative thinking. People don't last.

Life, for all that is invested in it, is a precarious business. Think of the months of preparation before a baby is born. Consider the years spent in preparing for adult life and the investment in education and training. Ponder on all the hopes people have and plans for their futures. And then think how precarious existence is.

You can walk across a road, hit a car and that's the end of you. You can be sitting on a plane, looking forward to visiting a foreign country, only suddenly to be sucked out into eternity by courtesy of a terrorist's bomb or a technical failure. You can make what you think will be a quite routine cross-Channel crossing, never to reach your destination. You can begin the day in a quite unexceptional way and plan all that's ahead of you, only to be struck down by a virus before you have had your coffee-break.

The Preacher is not so dramatic. 'Generations come and generations go.' Even without the unexpected he suggests that life is short enough. In the ordinary course of events we may live seventy, eighty or even ninety years. But then we will soon be forgotten and nobody will remember who we were.

As the Preacher was writing this, he may well have looked out across the mountains around Jerusalem, and that increased his sense of fragility. They were so massive, so solid, and had been there so long. They had been there years before his great great, great, great, great, grandfather – if he remembered who he was. Look at the great ocean depths, or the immense changelessness of the desert sands, or the rock we call planet Earth.

And what is man by comparison? Human beings come and go so quickly. We are like the temporary blip on a radar screen. Life is fleeting, transient, insubstantial, precarious, throwaway and disposable. How small it makes one feel.

Life is repetitive (1:5-7)
And that's a nightmare!

Mr Preacher introduces three illustrations from the natural world to make his point. First, think of the sun (*verse 5*). We might positively assert that 'from the rising of the sun, to the going down of the same, the Lord's name is to be praised'. But there is another way of looking at it. The Preacher says in effect, and in Charles Swindoll's memorable words, 'The rising of the sun – yuk!'[7]

Think how stupid it all is. The sun gets up in the morning and goes around its circuit like a runner that can't stop. Round and round and round and round.... It never seems to get to its destination; it never goes anywhere different; it never takes a holiday; it never goes in a different direction or into a different orbit. Day in and day out it is the same old thing. It is totally repetitive.

The wind (*verse 6*) seems just as bad. Where is it going to? And does it ever get to where it wants to go? It seems to go in any and all directions quite without reason. Not even the weather forecasters can explain the purpose of its journey. They can tell in advance where it is likely to go. And if they get it wrong, they can correct it the next day and announce where it went. They can even explain something of the patterns which cause it. But as for the purpose, aim and point of the ceaseless, restless blowing of the wind, they are ignorant. It creates havoc here, gently refreshes someone else there, returns with gale force somewhere else. It is tirelessly busy. But where is it going?

Then, what about the water? What a fascinating feature of our world. 'All streams flow into the sea, yet the sea is never full' (*verse 7*). It is as if the ocean is a gigantic bath in which the plug has been left out! So the water goes pouring in and pouring in but it never fills up. We know of course, the explanation. The water evaporates and so is recycled at a rate of a trillion tons a day into the atmosphere, only to descend to the earth again as rain. But that only highlights the Preacher's point. It is recycled. It must seem like serving a life-sentence on a treadmill without any hope of remission. 'Recycled' is only a posh word to disguise the tyrannical nature of repetitiveness.

The sun, wind and water only mirror our own experience. The monotony of lives condemned to repetition cause many to seek a way of escape.[8] Novelty seems to offer one escape route. So people change jobs, move house, buy gadgets or swap wives in an attempt to outmanoeuvre boredom.

Or, failing to make an outward change, they make a mental shift. So, the job in which they once invested so much significance now becomes peripheral to their thinking even while they keep doing it. They begin to find real meaning in a cause, or a hobby.... for a time, until that too loses its attraction.

Another strategy people adopt for coping with repetition is to escape into another world altogether, a world which is foreign to their own experience. The soap opera is a commonly accepted way of doing so and exists in ample quantities in our society. They can dream of the sunny climate of *Neighbours,* laugh at the antics and anxieties of *East Enders*, or rejoice that they are not trapped in the pettiness of *Coronation Street*.

In the end it makes little difference. Ordinary life is still the prime reality which has to be faced. And that is a repetitive nightmare.

Life is insatiable (1:8)
Few want to admit what their experience tells them. Life might be a monotonous drag but we are reluctant to accept that it is meant to be like that. Even if we agree with the Preacher that

'all things are wearisome, more than one can say', we always have an answer as to how we could change it.

Bath University once had a graffito scrawled on its wall which read, 'Do not adjust your life, the fault lies in reality.' The trouble is that we do not believe that. So, we argue, if only we had more recognition for what we do, earned better pay, got the promotion we deserved, had a more attractive husband or wife, lived in another part of town, had gone to a different school, then things would be different and we would be fulfilled. The fault lies in the circumstances of our lives and if they could be changed then reality would be fine.

The Preacher torpedoes that view with one missile. 'The eye never has enough of seeing, not the ear its fill of hearing.' Life has an appetite which can never be satisfied. Frankly, all the changes in the world would make no difference. Have you never noticed how we spend our lives saying that things will be different around the corner, but when we get there we find them just the same? The promotion comes, the recognition is given, the pay rise is in the bank, we move house and change our circumstances, but we are always hungry for more. Our commercial world is built on that assumption. Marketing people bank on it. That's why the advertisers know that they can convince us to purchase things we do not need. They want to replace yesterday's gadgets with today's toys. And they succeed in doing so because we are never satisfied. We think we will be, if only we had this latest thing or that. Yet when we've got them we are still left unsatisfied. They realize we shall never have enough.

Chuck Swindoll put it like this:

The itch for things, the lust for more – so brilliantly injected by those who peddle them – is a virus draining our souls of happy contentment. Have you noticed? A man never earns enough. A woman is never beautiful enough. Clothes are never fashionable enough. Cars are never nice enough. Gadgets are never modern enough. Houses are never furnished enough. Food is never fancy enough. Life is never full enough.[9]

That's quite a list! But it's true. Richard Foster has judged our desire for things 'psychotic'.[10] Surely he's right. It is out of touch with reality. It isn't rational because we know that when we have got more it will have changed nothing.

Life has a ravenous appetite which is never satisfied.

Life is unchangeable (1:9-10)
The French have a saying for it, *Plus ca change, plus ca meme chose*. (The more things change, the more things remain the same.)

We pride ourselves on living in a 'modern' society. Things are really improving. Technology is advancing, discoveries are being made, change is coming. But, alas, the more changes that we make the more we seem to be defeated in trying to change anything. It is not just that we think we have invented something new, only to be told by some condescending busybody that the Greeks did it that way centuries ago, or the ancient Chinese had it off to perfection, or some unheard-of civilization knew all about it. That is often the case, but the fear that things are unalterable is more fundamental than that.

The real problem is that none of our improvements really improve. We eradicate tuberculosis as a common cause of death, and thank God we do, only to encounter heart disease as a new, deadly and common enemy. We build highrise flats to provide people with accommodation and discover that having cured one set of social problems, those that result from homelessness or overcrowding, we have built in a new set of social problems which are even worse. We design new roads to ease the flow of traffic, only to find that all we have succeeded in doing is relocating the jam. We invent new systems to cope with society's problems only to find ourselves trapped by the same bureaucratic red tape or immovable vested interests as before.

Mr Preacher says there are no real surprises, no breakthroughs, no interventions which really alter anything. 'There is nothing new under the sun.'

Life is insignificant (1:11)

The Preacher now invites us to look back into history. We remember so little of it, if anything at all so important in its day, so vital, so impressive, so significant. But what does it matter now? Great people may have a page or two in the history books or even a biography or two. But most are simply forgotten. The heroes of yesterday are unheard of today.

The Preacher pessimistically forecasts that it will always be the same. We think that what we are engaged in is so memorable and of such moment, but within a generation people won't care and may not even have heard anything about us and our business.

It is a humbling thought. It occurs to me most when I go into a secondhand bookshop. Thousands of volumes lie there collecting dust and who really wants them? There is the occasional gem for which I've been searching for a long time. But the vast mass might lie there unsought and unbought for ever. But those books were the result of hard labour, years of effort, perhaps even a lifetime. They were the summit of someone's achievements. And yet now they lie unknown and unwanted. Sometimes you pick up an old volume and discover that the pages have never even been cut. They have never even been read. Was there any point in writing? Were they remembered a year after publication, five years, fifty years?

Isaac Watts captured it well:

> Time, like an ever-rolling stream
> Bears all her sons away.

People come and people go. Even the most significant in their day soon become insignificant.

Is that what life is really like? Boring, fragile, repetitive, insatiable, unalterable and insignificant? No wonder Blanche Dubois in *A Streetcar Named Desire* says, 'I don't want realism, I want magic.'[11] If that really is a true account of life, then surely it can only logically result in complete pessimism. Pessimism, in turn, would drive one to suicide or to mindless acceptance of the system – the equivalent of becoming conformist and institutionalized in prison – simply as a strategy to lessen the pain and to secure release as early and unscathed as possible.

But the Preacher is not ready to give in to pessimism so easily. He has the niggling feeling that what he has described is not quite the whole story. Twice within these verses he refers to this as life 'under the sun' (*verses 3 and 9*). He has talked of life purely from a horizontal viewpoint. It is a secularist's picture of it that he has painted. It is what the world is like without God anywhere to be seen.

So he begins to ponder. Is there anything beyond the sun which might have an influence or cause us to alter our perspective? Is there no other reality which would enable us to rise above the down-drag of life? Is there no transcendent dimension which can help?

Perhaps. But Mr Preacher is not going to jump to glib conclusions and assert that there must be a God over it all. All he knows is that if you do rule out the possibility of God, life makes no sense.

A contemporary sociologist has reached the same conclusion. Peter Berger, far from accepting that our world will become increasingly secular until, with a fatal inevitability, no-one believes in God, argues that secularization will have the brakes put on it before long. Why?

Because, he says:

> I am impressed by the intrinsic inability of secularized world views to answer the deeper questions of the human condition, questions of whence, wither and why. These seem to be ineradicable and they are answered only in the most banal ways by the ersatz religions of secularism. Perhaps, finally, the reversibility of the process of secularization is probable because of the pervasive boredom of a world without gods.[12]

Exactly! That's just what the Preacher has been trying to say. Secularism can only produce a life which is profoundly unsatisfying. 'Life under the sun' is a monotonous, meaningless wisp of vapour.

But perhaps after all there is something or someone above the sun which would make all the difference in the world.

References
1. Stanley Cohen and Laurie Taylor, *Escape Attempts: The Theory and Practice of Resistance to Everyday Life* (Penguin, 1978), p. 45.
2. Robert Davidson, *The Courage of Doubt* (SCM, 1983), p. 202.
3. Derek Kidner, *The Message of Ecclesiastes* (IVP, 1976), p. 22.
4. Quoted by Cohen and Taylor, p.27.
5. Quoted by David Bleakley, *Work: The Shadow and the Substance* (SCM, 1983), p. 35.
6. Peter Williamson and Kevin Perrotta (eds), *Christianity Confronts Modernity* (Handsel Press, 1981), p. 52.
7. Charles R. Swindoll, *Living on the Ragged Edge* (Word, 1986), p.29.
8. See Cohen and Taylor, pp 46-137.
9. Swindoll, p. 21.
10. Richard Foster, *Celebration of Discipline* (Hodder & Stoughton, 1980), p.70.
11. Cohen and Taylor, p. 69.
12. Peter L. Berger, *Facing Up To Modernity* (Penguin, 1979), p. 201.

2

CHASING THE WIND
1:12 – 2:26

[12]I, the Teacher, was king over Israel in Jerusalem. [13]I devoted myself to study and to explore by wisdom all that is done under heaven. What a heavy burden God has laid on men! [14]I have seen all the things that are done under the sun; all of them are meaningless, a chasing after the wind.

[15]What is twisted cannot be straightened;
    what is lacking cannot be counted.

[16]I thought to myself, "Look, I have grown and increased in wisdom more than anyone who has ruled over Jerusalem before me; I have experienced much of wisdom and knowledge." [17]Then I applied myself to the understanding of wisdom, and also of madness and folly, but I learned that this, too, is a chasing after the wind.

[18]For with much wisdom comes much sorrow;
    the more knowledge, the more grief.

[1]I thought in my heart, "Come now, I will test you with pleasure to find out what is good." But that also proved to be meaningless. [2]"Laughter," I said, "is foolish. And what does pleasure accomplish?" [3]I tried cheering myself with wine, and embracing folly – my mind still guiding me with wisdom. I wanted to see what was worth while for men to do under heaven during the few days of their lives.

[4]I undertook great projects: I built houses for myself and planted vineyards. [5]I made gardens and parks and planted all kinds of fruit trees in them. [6]I made reservoirs to water groves of flourishing trees. [7]I bought male and female slaves and had other slaves who were born in my house. I also owned more herds and flocks than anyone in Jerusalem before me. [8]I amassed silver and gold for myself, and the treasure of kings and provinces. I acquired men and women singers, and a harem as well – the delights of the heart of man. [9]I became greater by far than anyone in Jerusalem before me. In all this my wisdom stayed with me.

22

[10]I denied myself nothing my eyes desired;
    I refused my heart no pleasure.
My heart took delight in all my work,
    and this was the reward for all my labour.
[11]Yet when I surveyed all that my hands had done
    and what I had toiled to achieve,
everything was meaningless, a chasing after the wind;
    nothing was gained under the sun.
[12]Then I turned my thoughts to consider wisdom,
    and also madness and folly.
What more can the king's successor do
    than what has already been done?
[13]I saw that wisdom is better than folly,
    just as light is better than darkness.
[14]The wise man has eyes in his head,
    while the fool walks in the darkness;
but I came to realise
    that the same fate overtakes them both.
[15]Then I thought in my heart,

"The fate of the fool will overtake me also.
    What then do I gain by being wise?"
I said in my heart,
    "This too is meaningless."
[16]For the wise man, like the fool, will not be long remembered;
    in days to come both will be forgotten.
Like the fool, the wise man too must die!

[17]So I hated life, because the work that is done under the sun was grievous to me. All of it is meaningless, a chasing after the wind. [18]I hated all the things I had toiled for under the sun, because I must leave them to the one who comes after me. [19]And who knows whether he will be a wise man or a fool? Yet he will have control over all the work into which I have poured my effort and skill under the sun. This too is meaningless. [20]So my heart began to despair over all my toilsome labour under the sun. [21]For a man may do his work with wisdom, knowledge and skill, and then he must leave all he owns to someone who has not worked for it. This too is meaningless and a great misfortune. [22]What does a man get for all the toil and anxious striving with which he labours

under the sun? [23]All his days his work is pain and grief; even at night his mind does not rest. This too is meaningless.

[24]A man can do nothing better than to eat and drink and find satisfaction in his work. This too, I see, is from the hand of God, [25]for without him, who can eat or find enjoyment? [26]To the man who pleases him, God gives wisdom, knowledge and happiness, but to the sinner he gives the task of gathering and storing up wealth to hand it over to the one who pleases God. This too is meaningless, a chasing after the wind.

'Tell me,' said the cynic to the sociologist, 'as a non-participant observer, what do you think of the human race?' No cynic could ever accuse Mr Preacher, the author of Ecclesiastes, of being a non-participant observer. He wanted to know the purpose of life and, in order to discover it, he threw himself into life with zest. He refused to take the question of life's purpose lying down. He was not going to let it gnaw away at him like a steady, nagging toothache rather than face the fear of going to the dentist. He was happy to encounter and to discover the worst, as long as the question could be answered.

His determination to resolve the problem led him to engage in exhaustive study and copious experimentation (1:13). Furthermore he was going to find out at first hand. He shunned the life of the ivory tower academic. He was not going to observe from a distance. Nor was he going to be a mere critic, commenting on what others had done but never having the courage to do it himself. So he got into everything and explored every conceivable option. His investigation was thorough.

Looking for meaning: the conclusions (1:13-15)

With typical Jewish provocation he again gives us the conclusions before setting out the data which justifies them. In a few words he complains, 'What a heavy burden God has laid on men! I have seen all the things that are done under the sun, all of them are meaningless, a chasing after the wind' (1:13-14). More fully, he reaches three conclusions.

Life is futile

For all the experiments he has conducted his results are nil. He can tell us that the clue to life doesn't lie in this direction, or in that, or in the other. But he can't tell us where it does lie. There seems to be no answer.

Perhaps that's some gain. Thomas Edison conducted 50,000 experiments, all of which failed, before inventing a new storage battery. When someone commented to him on his lack of results he replied, 'Results, why I have gotten a lot of results. I know fifty thousand things that won't work.'[1] That's about where the Preacher is too. He can tell you where you *won't* find the answer, and I suppose that's progress. But he cannot tell you where you *will* find the answer.

So his first disappointing conclusion is that finding the meaning of life is like 'chasing after wind'. Have you ever tried to capture the wind and put it in a bottle to preserve it? It just cannot be done. It's a nonsense. It's a vivid picture of a futile quest and that just about sums up the Preacher's feelings on searching for the purpose of life.

Life is twisted

Mr Preacher has more to say. 'What is twisted cannot be straightened; what is lacking cannot be counted' (1:15). For all his erudition the Preacher is unable to make any sense of what he sees. Life's anomalies cannot be straightened out nor life's experiences reduced to a neat system. He does not think that the fault lies in his own shortcomings. Rather he doubts whether there are any answers. If there are then they are unobtainable by human beings.

Life seems like one of those tantalizing wooden puzzles, odd shaped bits of which you have to piece together to make a perfect square or sphere. Time and again you think you just discovered the secret only to be disappointed. You think all the bits are in place at last and will hold together, only for it to fall apart in your hands once more. If there is a solution no-one has let you in on the secret.

Life is cursed
The Preacher is convinced that God is to blame for all this. It isn't just that we feel as if we are carrying around a load of luggage on our backs, the real aggravation is that God has condemned us to do so (*verse 13*). We want to protest and say it is not fair. There may well be some reason for it, but at the moment it is not the reason but the reality of it which concerns the Preacher most.

A few chapters later (3:9-11) the Preacher begins to venture a reason. It is God's way of reminding us that a world where he has been left out simply cannot function as it should nor can people be happy in it. The irritation and wearisomeness of life is God's strategy to remind us of our need for him.

Paul acknowledged the same annoying facts of life. 'The creation,' he wrote, 'was subjected to frustration, not by its own choice, but by the will of the one who subjected it' (Rom. 8:20). But Paul can see a little more and adds that the world was subjected to frustration 'in hope'. He was able to see God's cosmic plan of bringing everything back into its proper relationship with him. If everything were fine now, if there were no problems, either in our own lives or in the world generally, then we would never turn to God. We'd feel that we had no need for him. It is sad, but true, that many make the acquaintance of God only when trouble strikes or failure comes their way.

But all this is to put the cart before the horse. What were his experiments which led him to such negative results?

Looking for meaning through wisdom (1:16-18)

If the Preacher is telling Solomon's story, as we believe he is, albeit in the first person, it is natural that he should begin his search for meaning by reference to wisdom. 1 Kings 3:4-15 tells us how important Solomon considered wisdom to be. And, Solomon could rightly make the claim of verse 16, 'Look, I have grown and increased in wisdom more than anyone who has ruled over Jerusalem before me; I have experienced much of wisdom and knowledge.'

He speaks for many who say that life makes no sense simply because we do not know enough to make sense of it. If only we could research more, discover more, think more deeply or be more discerning, then we would understand and our problems would be solved. But Solomon was a man who had the mental equipment and opportunity to think at a profound level and if anyone should have been able to resolve the riddle of life it should have been him. He ran though the whole gamut of philosophy, wisdom and speculation that was available and his verdict was that it solved nothing.

In verse 17, the Preacher is keen to forestall a possible accusation against Solomon. Some might say that the trouble with Solomon was that he did not have a genuinely open mind. He went into his investigation determined to find certain answers. But, the Preacher says, Solomon applied himself 'to the understanding of wisdom, and also of madness and folly'. While it is true that he expected to find the answers down a particular pathway, he nonetheless examined the alternatives when he failed to do so. While he thought the answer would lie in the direction of wisdom he was open to the possibility that the answer might lie instead in madness and folly.

Some schools of psychiatry see madness and folly as a perfectly rational way of coping with our peculiar world. So much so that some question what is normal and who really is mad. R.D. Laing, for example, writes in his Preface to *The Divided Self*, 'In the context of our present pervasive madness that we call normality, sanity, freedom, all our frames of reference are ambiguous and equivocal.'[2] In other words, you can never be sure who is sane and who is insane, what is normal and what is abnormal. The definitions are not that clear.

Solomon was prepared to give it a go. But he did not find that such a road yielded any more answers than did the conventional one.

All in all, Solomon's search has ended in failure. He concludes that the more you understand, the less you understand; the more you peer into the mystery, the more out of focus it becomes; the more you think you have things under control, the more things jump out at you. James Moffatt brilliantly translated Solomon's conclusion in verse 18 as, 'The more you understand the more you ache.'

I admire the schoolteacher who had the courage to write on a boy's report, 'If ignorance is bliss, your son is going to have a very happy life.' Solomon, in effect, confirms that ignorance is bliss and wishes he knew a little less.

Ultimately, those who engage in more recent forms of philosophical speculation reach the same verdict. Helpful though philosophy may be in unravelling a certain order of questions, it fails to give conclusive answers to the questions of the meaning of life. Its very fashions show philosophy's provisional nature as it rejects linguistic analysis in favour of existentialism or Marxism, only for them to be overthrown by even later fads. Philosophy, like the wisdom of which Solomon spoke, is a 'no through road' if we want to use it as a route to the meaning of life.

Perhaps the trouble for Solomon lay in his understanding of wisdom. Elsewhere he was clear that 'the fear of the LORD was the beginning of wisdom' (Prov. 9:10). Here he has no such definition. God has been left out. He has changed his starting-point. No wonder he never reaches his destination.

Looking for meaning through pleasure (2:1-11)
If philosophy and wisdom are not your cup of tea then pleasure may well be. It is a much more promising approach for the average person who might well have told him, if he had asked, that his search for meaning through wisdom would be unprofitable. What did he expect? Real life surely begins when work and the serious stuff is over. It is in enjoyment, when people are mentally disengaged, that they really find themselves.

But immediately we run into a catch. The Preacher has to admit that in conducting this set of experiments, what you end up testing is not so much the various forms of pleasure which are on offer, as yourself and your own reaction to them. That's why he says, 'Come now, I will test you with pleasure to find out what is good' (*verse 1*). He realizes that he can peer into particular pleasures only to discover he's looking in a mirror and staring at himself. One man's meat is another man's poison. The same is true of pleasure. So the Preacher, still reporting on Solomon's experience in the first person, investigates a wide range of pleasure. There's something here for everyone.

Laughter (2:2)
If the meaning of life is not to be found down a serious path perhaps it can be found down a comic one. Just accept life as it is and don't take it too seriously for that will only lead to problems. Rather see the funny side and learn to laugh at life, and fulfilment will come. Laughter is the best medicine.

But the moment we are invited to follow this path we know

it to be a fraud. Many of the greatest comics, who have caused millions to laugh, have themselves been so deeply unhappy. There was no greater comedian in recent decades than Tony Hancock. At the height of his fame, in 1961, he was entertaining fifteen and a half million people, 30% of the adult population of the United Kingdom, every week, with *Hancock's Half Hour*. Can anyone who saw or heard him ever forget *The Blood Donor* or *The Radio Ham*? He not only reduced the population of the United Kingdom to mass hilarity but he was frequently reduced to tears of laughter himself. He was a superb artist and comic.

Yet in 1968 he committed suicide. In his personal life he had been deeply unhappy for years, always striving to understand himself and yet never doing so. It was a tragic end to a brilliant life. His biographer writes:

> It may be that Hancock eventually managed to see himself in the cosmic perspective he had sought for years, as an insignificant speck of dust in an obscure corner of the universe, end product of a long line of accidental survivals. It is one thing to talk about the need for perspective; it must be unbearable to find it.[3]

'He had no faith himself and acted as if he were the first man to discover doubt.'[4] He frequently talked long into the night with friends about the purpose of existence and whether there was any pattern discernible in human progress. But he would accept no answers, believing that the very questions themselves were unanswerable. When Kenneth Williams suggested that faith would explain the apparent meaninglessness, Tony Hancock rejected the idea on the grounds that it was unprovable.

Spike Milligan said of him, 'One by one he shut the door on all the people he knew; then he shut the door on himself.'[5] So much for laughter.

The pleasures of the community

In the same verse the Preacher uses the word 'pleasure' to speak about a more thoughtful approach to finding satisfaction. 'Pleasure' speaks about those good wholesome occasions of enjoyment which every community has: the festivals, the street parties, the carnivals, the fetes and garden parties, the firework displays and all sorts of public celebrations. He has a royal wedding or a national anniversary or a victory celebration in mind.

Comedy may be an exclusive form of pleasure. It appeals to some but leaves others cold. Furthermore it too quickly degenerates to the borderline or depends on a sense of the absurd. But community celebrations are inclusive and wholesome. Everyone is sucked into the rejoicing except a few isolated individuals who have never integrated into the community. It's a form of pleasure where everyone has a place. It is open and above board. It makes people feel they belong and uplifts the spirits of all but the most hardened cynics.

It is the absence of community with its sense of belonging and fun and its replacement by a much more impersonal society which many blame for our ills today. A return to former days, we are told, would quickly bring us a sense of direction and purpose and overcome our discontents. If only we still made our own entertainment as in the good old days when we sang around the piano instead of getting it ready-made and packaged from the television or the computer!

But the Preacher protests that this would not improve things as much as we like to think. For all the enjoyment of such pleasures, he asks, what do they really accomplish? Do they really do anything to fill the empty aching heart? They may temporarily relieve the symptoms but they never cure the disease.

Alcohol (2:3)

Next comes a brief excursion into alcohol. That too might lift his spirits a bit! All he did was get a little merry. He tells us that he didn't allow himself to go too far down this road and end up as an alcoholic in a semi-permanent stupour. But he went far enough to relax the control on his senses and 'embrace folly'.

But that's no answer. It's just sheer escapism. The bottle may make the drinker feel a little different but the world, reality, life, call it what you will, is unaffected. Should the imbiber ever have the misfortune to be stone-cold sober again he quickly realizes that nothing has changed.

Worthwhile activity (2:4-6)

A new set of experiments is set up in the area of pleasure. This time Solomon wants to see if there is meaning in something more substantial and worthwhile. Like many a rich person he decided to use his resources creatively. He would ensure that his mark was left behind him when he went. So he erected buildings, planted vineyards, created gardens, established parks and, wisely, if any of those things were to survive in the climate in which he lived, he dug reservoirs. That irrigation system even allowed him to invest in forestry with minimum financial risks.

What a terrific achievement! No doubt others admired it as solid and lasting. No doubt it provided him with some satisfaction, the more so because he was clearly able to benefit others through his projects. Yet he does not linger over the satisfaction. He speeds on, like a machine that has gone into overdrive, in his relentless pursuit of meaning. Perhaps, after all, he did not find what he was looking for in his feats of architecture, engineering and agriculture. He seems to have that awful feeling of anticlimax. Like Bob Geldof, at the end of the day, he asks, 'Is that it?'

Why didn't he find meaning here? Derek Kidner provides a clue. He notes that there is no mention of God in any of these projects. He builds his own house, but seems indifferent to the house of the Lord. It is an 'under the sun' perspective. Kidner writes: 'He creates a little world within a world: multiform, harmonious, exquisite: a secular Garden of Eden, full of civilized and agreeably uncivilized delights, with no forbidden fruits – or none which he regards as such.'[6] But can any attempt to create one's own world – a world where nothing is forbidden and God is ignored – ever be anything other than desperately unsatisfying?

Power (2:7-8)

Nothing sets the adrenalin running so much as being able to exercise power. The temptations of power seduce us all. It ensnares the school bully and the school prefect; the thug and the high-ranking police officer; the car-park attendant and the Whitehall mandarin, the pew-filler and the preacher. Paul Tournier, the Christian psychiatrist, recognized its hold over us. 'The simple fact is that we are all moved without knowing it by an imperious will to power which brooks no obstacle.'[7] It certainly got Solomon, as the Preacher in Ecclesiastes relates.

He may have had more right to it than most of us. But he certainly exploited those rights to the full. Three types of power are mentioned.

First, he has *power over people*. He talks of slaves (*verse 7*), some of whom he bought and others of whom were born into his household. What power he exercised over them! Ultimately he had the power of life and death over them. But without being so drastic he could order them to do his every whim and punish them if they refused. He could use them or abuse them. That was power!

Secondly, he had *power through property*. His farms (*verse 7*) were better stocked than any that had gone before. Think of the implications of that. He could corner the meat market, control the price of cattle and regulate the employment situation. An essential ally of all that was power through money (*verse 8*). Elsewhere we learn that gold and silver were as common in Solomon's time as stone (2 Chr. 9:27). He was the regular J.R. Ewing of his day, though not necessarily as nasty! Here was economic power!

Thirdly, he exercised *power through sex* (*verse 8*). According to 1 Kings 11:3 Solomon had 700 wives and 300 concubines and they didn't do him any good. Sex is a powerful weapon in our attempt to exploit and dominate others. The rapist, the child abuser and the pornography merchant demonstrate that in its most extreme forms. But it happens on a perfectly normal level, in a thousand subtle ways too. In this Solomon simply had more experience than most of us.

Assessment (2:9-10)

Before the preacher sets out his conclusion from all these experiments in pleasure, he enters two qualifications. First, for all the forms of pleasure he explored, Solomon never lost his scientific objectivity. 'In all this my wisdom stayed with me' (*verse 9*). So the conclusions reached were trustworthy. Secondly, his researches had been comprehensive (*verse 10*). He had denied himself nothing and entered into everything fully. No stone was left unturned. So the conclusion should be worth listening to.

The morning after the night before, when he had time to reflect on all these pleasures in which he had indulged, he came to a shattering conclusion. However worthwhile some of them may have been in themselves, none of them unlocked the secret of the meaning or purpose in life. 'I realized that it didn't mean a thing. It was like chasing after the wind' (*verse 11, GNB*). He had everything he wanted and had attained some notable achievements, but they left him empty.

Looking for meaning through traditional values (2:12-16)
So the relentless quest continues. The Preacher returns to re-examine wisdom. Wisdom, this time, is not of the speculative philosophical kind but of the down-to-earth, good, old-fashioned, practical kind. It's about the traditional values which were embedded in society and which had not served their ancestors too badly. Former generations had not appeared restless and unfulfilled, as the Preacher apparently was, so perhaps there was some mileage to be found there.

What does he have in mind that can make such a difference? Traditional teaching about wisdom would have included such topics as how to show respect for your neighbour, how to avoid evil, how to control your tongue, the value of hard work, of listening to others, of planning and time-keeping and of keeping a right perspective regarding suffering and poverty. All very good. Of course it naturally led to a way of life which was more sensible than one where all that sound teaching was ignored.

The Preacher readily acknowledges that there is value to be found there. It 'is better than folly' (*verse 13*) for the simple reason that it enables a person to walk in the light rather than stumble in darkness. That must be good. Who, in their right mind, would want to live in a perpetual night?

That's fine! But then the Preacher thinks of the bottom line. The fact of the matter is, he says, that it doesn't really matter how you live in the long run because 'the same fate overtakes' both the wise and the fool (*verse 14*). As George Bernard Shaw put it, 'Death is the ultimate statistic; one out of one will die.' Then the Preacher finds his mind trapped by that depressing thought, unable to escape. He muses on the morbid destination that wise and foolish alike share (*verses 15-16*).

Once again he finds himself asking, What's the point? The wise person may have kept every rule in the book, and he may even have known his way around the wisdom writings like the back of his hand, only to go exactly the same way as the biggest buffoon around.

In days to come they will both be forgotten. Short memories begin the day they die. The wise person might have a brilliant funeral with a generous oration that lasts all of fifteen minutes. Of course it leaves a lot out. Compressing a lifetime into fifteen minutes is bound to make the orator selective! Then the coffin is lowered into the ground and that's it. A few minutes later exactly the same ritual is followed for the fool. Selective memories get into gear once more. People are too polite to be too honest at funeral services. Perhaps he wasn't so bad after all. Then he too is lowered into the ground and forgotten. *Finis.*

So, the Preacher concludes, there might be some limited value in observing traditional teaching regarding wisdom but that is superficial in relation to the depth of question he's asking. It will make it a little easier to get on with others in this life. But, in the face of death, it is really quite trivial. From that standpoint we see that memories are too short to make any human endeavour worth while.

Looking for meaning through hard work (2:17-23)
The pendulum swings back again. The Preacher is now on the rebound from his philosophizing. Life is too short to allow the luxury of thinking. The answer must lie in getting stuck in. Life is too brief to allow the luxury of pleasure-seeking. There's too much that needs doing. So get on with it. Life is

too short to spend it debating whether traditional values are going to lead you anywhere or not. Just get involved. The people with the problems are people with time on their hands. A good dose of hard work is the answer. That is how you will discover meaning in life without ever asking the question.

The case is still argued. 'Bring back conscription,' they say. 'Force the unemployed into community work. That'll soon solve our nation's problems.' Mrs Thatcher, 'preaching a sermon' on Ash Wednesday in 1981, said as much. She combined the need for work with the need for a revival of traditional values.

> There is one other characteristic of our nation which is, I think, worth mentioning: we have always had a sense that work is not only a necessity, it is a duty, and indeed a virtue. It is an expression of our dependence on each other. Work is not merely a way of receiving a pay packet but a means whereby everyone in the community benefits and society is enriched.... If I am right, we need to establish in the minds of young and old alike a national purpose which has a real meaning for them. It must include the defence of the values which we believe to be of vital importance. Unless the spirit of the nation is renewed, our national way of life will perish.[8]

The Preacher is not so easily taken in by all this talk about the virtues of hard work. He can see through it for a number of reasons. One, when you die you have to leave it all to someone else (*verse 18*). Two, you cannot be sure whether he will look after it or ruin it (*verse 19*). Three, you have no choice but to give it away as a gift to someone who has not worked for it (*verse 21*). Four, what benefit did you derive from it? Honesty would compel you to answer that the debit column, full as it is with items like ulcers and sleepless nights, adds up to more than the credit column.

By now the Preacher is being pushed beyond his normal

conclusions. So far he has drawn a blank in his search for meaning but he has not given up hope that he might find the answer eventually. Now, however, he comes to despair (*verse 20*). Using the phrase 'under the sun', the code words for the godless perspective, he now concludes that wherever you look, wherever you experiment, life is empty, futile, meaningless, cursed and twisted. It's like chasing the wind.

Finding meaning through God (2:24-26)
Having been driven into a godless corner, the Preacher begins to fight back. The mood changes. An oasis is seen in the desert.

At first sight he seems to be repeating what he has just rejected. He tells us to 'eat, drink and find satisfaction in ... work' (*verse 24*) and not to neglect wisdom and knowledge (*verse 26*). If the ultimate meaning of life is not found in these things neither is it to be found in rejecting them. It is not wisdom, pleasure, the traditional value system or work which provides meaning in and of itself. What matters is your understanding of them.

Previously he had left God out. It was an account of life 'under the sun'. He explored everything 'under heaven'. Wisdom began with him. His perspective on pleasure was totally self-centred. 'I built houses for myself'(*verse 4*). 'I denied myself nothing' (*verse 10*).

Now God is brought into the picture and things begin to change. It's like a number of television commercials. Everything is grey and drab, portrayed in the old unexciting black and white, until the product appears. Then suddenly the colour and life return. So it is with God. Satisfaction will be found through eating and drinking or any other material thing only when it is realized that they are 'from the hand of God'. Happiness will be found through 'wisdom and knowledge' only when it is understood that they too are a gift from God.

Contentment is a gift of God which comes independent of your outward circumstances. Without it, life is a curse. With it, the believer can enjoy life to the full (1 Tim. 4:4; 6:6-8)

So the choice is ours. The Preacher concludes by saying that there are two paths from which we must choose. We may choose to please God (*verse 26*) and find meaning, purpose and fulfilment, seeing life as an incredible gift from God and living it with humility and thankfulness. It will not mean that there will never be disappointments, let-downs and failures. They will still come. But knowing that God remains in control, even of those, makes us see them in a different light. Deep down there will be trust and contentment.

The alternative is to go the way of the sinner (*verse 26*). That simply is the way which leaves God out. It is the way of the unbeliever, of the person who refuses to trust in God. Take that road if you like but read the warning first. It's a blind alley. All that you will be left with is your paltry projects, your emptiness, plus.... nothing. Such a life is like chasing after the wind.

Which route are you taking?

References
1. Clifton Fadiman (ed), *The Faber Book of Anecdotes* (Faber, 1985), p. 183.
2. R.D. Laing, *The Divided Self* (Penguin, 1996), p. 11.
3. Freddie Hancock and David Nathan, *Hancock* (BBC Publications, 1986), p. 191.
4. *Ibid.*, p. 81.
5. *Ibid.*, p. 81.
6. Derek Kidner, *The Message of Ecclesiastes* (IVP, 1976), p. 32.
7. Quoted by Cheryl Forbes, *The Religion of Power* (Marc, 1986), p.15.
8. Margaret Thatcher, The Spirit of the Nation, *Third Way* (May, 1981), p. 15.

3

TIME AND ETERNITY
3:1-22

There is a time for everything,
> and a season for every activity under heaven:
> ^{2} a time to be born and a time to die,
> a time to plant and a time to uproot,
> ^{3} a time to kill and a time to heal,
> a time to tear down and a time to build,
> ^{4} a time to weep and a time to laugh,
> a time to mourn and a time to dance,
> ^{5} a time to scatter stones and a time to gather them,
> a time to embrace and a time to refrain,
> ^{6} a time to search and a time to give up,
> a time to keep and a time to throw away,
> ^{7} a time to tear and a time to mend,
> a time to be silent and a time to speak,
> ^{8} a time to love and a time to hate,
> a time for war and a time for peace.

^{9}What does the worker gain from his toil? ^{10}He has made everything beautiful in its time. I have seen the burden God has laid on men. ^{11}He has also set eternity in the hearts of men; yet they cannot fathom what God has done from beginning to end. ^{12}I know that there is nothing better for men than to be happy and do good while they live. ^{13}That everyone may eat and drink, and find satisfaction in all his toil – this is the gift of God. ^{14}I know that everything God does will endure for ever; nothing can be added to it and nothing taken from it. God does it so that men will revere him.

> ^{15}Whatever is has already been,
> and what will be has been before;
> and God will call the past to account.

^{16}And I saw something else under the sun:

40

In the place of judgment – wickedness was there, in the
place of justice – wickedness was there.

[17]I thought in my heart,

"God will bring to judgment
both the righteous and the wicked,
for there will be a time for every activity,
a time for every deed."

[18]I also thought, "As for men, God tests them so that they may see
that they are like the animals. [19]Man's fate is like that of the animals;
the same fate awaits them both: As one dies, so dies the other. All
have the same breath; man has no advantage over the animal.
Everything is meaningless. [20]All go to the same place; all come from
dust, and to dust all return. [21]Who knows if the spirit of man rises upward
and if the spirit of the animal goes down into the earth?" [22]So I saw that
there is nothing better for a man than to enjoy his work, because that is
his lot. For who can bring him to see what will happen after him?

Dave Clark's musical *Time* played to packed houses in
London. The story line was thin. 'Now that man is venturing
to the stars and has already walked on the Moon, "Melchi-
sedec", the Time Lord, has decided that the time has come to
examine the Earth's people to determine whether they shall
be an asset or a threat to universal peace. The time is now.'

A mix-up occurs. Instead of the world's rulers being
transported to the courtroom of the universe, a bunch of rock
musicians get sent there by mistake. They have to answer for
the world, and have a real struggle in trying to do so. They
can only trot out feeble excuses for man's absurd way of
treating his fellow human beings. 'Give us time,' they plead.
'Time will teach us all.' The Judges, Trigon, Lagus and
Morgua, take some convincing, and in the end it's a feeble
mixture of trust, sentiment and an exercise of mercy on the
part of Akash, 'the Ultimate Word in Truth', that grants the
earth a reprieve.

The show was savaged by the critics. One of them commented that 'Time was the one thing it didn't have' and promptly forecast it would be closed within weeks. His prediction proved untrue. The show continued a long time, saved perhaps by the brilliant sound sensations and visual effects that the audience experience and by the lead performance of Cliff Richard, that apparently eternal youth.

Yet, there is something too which intrigues us about the theme.

Time Waits For Nobody

> We must all plan our hopes together
> Or we'll have no future at all
> Time waits for nobody
> Time waits for nobody
> Time waits for nobody

So ran the recurring theme song. It's a plea for international peace. 'We've got to build up this world together or we'll have no future at all.' 'We've got to trust in one another or we'll have no future at all.' There is the recognition that when it comes to time we are not in control. Time is our master. It is set on its unstoppable course.

Time exercises a curious hold over us. It's shrouded in mystery. What exactly is it? Can we beat it? Why can't we travel backwards or project ourselves into the future? It's surrounded by myths. 'Time heals,' we say, knowing that sometimes it doesn't do anything of the sort. 'We've all the time in the world,' some boast; while others 'haven't got time'. We can be behind the times or have time on our hands. It's tyrannical. Byron called it 'the avenger'. It certainly doesn't give. Like money we can spend it any way we want but we can only spend it once. It never comes back again though we sometimes wish it would.

Time is full of potential. Nothing is more even-handed than time. The President of the USA and the President of Russia have no more time than you and I. The busy industrialist has no more time than the drifter; the creative artist whose work is prolific has no more time than the dropout. All have exactly the same amount of time in a day.

No commentary on life would be complete without some reflection on time, and Ecclesiastes provides us with one of the most famous reflections on it of all time.

Time – Poetry and Providence (3:1-8)
Here is sheer poetry! We feel the impact of the words as we read them. But what do they mean?

There are two ways of understanding what the Preacher says. He might be saying that time is a tyrant and, therefore, so is the God who stands behind it. Life is in a constant state of change over which many have no control. It is for ever catching people on the hop and making them feel insecure. Human experience is frustrating because time imposes itself on people as an arbitrary ruler and there is nothing they can do to fight back. People think they are in control of their circumstances only for something to happen just at that moment which results in sudden change to all their plans. If this view is correct then the poetry is tragic. It is a further reason for the Preacher to plunge into despair. Life is seen as nothing more than 'doing time'.

But there are good reasons for doubting that this is the right way to look at these verses. When we take into account the whole sweep of the chapter, and especially verses 11-15, it is more likely that the Preacher is saying that time is not a tyrant but a blessing. Here is a celebration of variety of life, all of which happens under the providential care of God. The poetry is not inviting us to protest against the tyranny of God but rather to rejoice in the providence of God.

Thank God for variety. If life were unchanged think how much more monotonous it would be than it already is. We think we would like to live in a perpetual summer but in reality we're glad of the changing seasons. Each of them has its own special attractions, its distinctive colours, smells and atmosphere. What a creative God he is to have thought of such subtle changes as the seasons which would have such far-reaching effect.

Thank God for providence. If we read verses 1-8 through the lens of verses 11-15 this becomes the dominant thought. God presides in love over all the circumstances of our lives. From where we are we may not always be able to understand what is happening to us. As Soren Kierkegaard put it, 'Life has to be lived forwards, the trouble is that we can only understand it backwards.' There are times when we cry out in real desperation, 'Why has God allowed this to happen to me?' We accuse him of messing up our plans, of dashing our cherished hopes and sometimes of being plain mean. But then, when we've lived life forwards, we stand and look back and see there was sense in it after all.

That sense is possible because we are not the playthings of some impersonal fate but the creatures of a loving Creator whom we can know as 'Father'.

It is from that standpoint that the Preacher muses on time. His thoughts range over everything in life from its most momentous events to its trivial pursuits.

Creation and destruction (3:3-4)

Starting with the most fundamental illustrations of this to be seen in birth and death, he immediately reminds us of how little is in our control. We did not negotiate with our parents the day when we should be born, nor did they negotiate it with anyone else. They may have 'planned' their family but in practice there were so many things beyond their control that our arrival in the world was out of their hands. So it is with death. It comes to some before they want it, while others, like aged saints who long to 'go home', are kept waiting. It is unpredictable.

He is not only concerned about the fact that such things are beyond our control but that both birth and death are appropriate in their setting. That same appropriate rhythm of granting and withdrawing life is seen elsewhere: in the garden and the fields ('a time to plant and a time to uproot'), among the nations and in the area of social relationships ('a time to kill and a time to heal') and even on the building site ('a time to tear down and a time to build'). There are times when it is right to do the one and equally times when it is right to do the other.

Joy and sorrow (3:4)
There is a variety in our human emotions and again it is appropriate that this should be so. The person for whom life is a bundle of fun from beginning to end is too good to be true. Not only must he be enormously insensitive to others who have a real reason to be sad, but he himself misses out on so many of the deeper lessons that pain and sorrow alone can teach us.

But the person who never laughs or dances is equally missing out. Within such a person there is often a shy and lonely being, fearfully locked up, longing for release and wanting to reach out to others and share in their pleasures but unable to do so.

Both laughter and sorrow are appropriate in their place and it is an idiot or a sorry individual who cannot distinguish between the two.

Friendship and enmity (3:5)

It is not immediately clear what the Preacher means by scattering stones and gathering them. Some say that it is a Jewish way of talking about love. But even if it is not that specific it is almost certainly talking about the general area of making friends and enemies. The line that runs parallel with it would suggest that this is the best way to understand it. If you scattered stones over a neighbour's field you would be making the field unproductive and causing him a lot of hard work. You would also almost certainly be making an enemy of him. On the other hand if you gathered stones you would be helping him out, expressing friendship and making his field more suitable to use.

Relationships need to be of different kinds. The person who wants to be a friend of God will not make friends of God's enemies (Ps. 1:1; Jas. 4:4). There is a time to express disapproval as well as to express approval.

In the variety of our friendships we also need to remember that relationships need to be of different degrees of intensity and intimacy. The most intimate relationship is to be found between two people of opposite sexes in marriage. No other relationship can, or should, ever be that close. We also need to relate to a small group of friends to an extent which goes beyond anything we can manage with a larger group. We need to sense the appropriateness of the relationship for each situation and not imagine that we will always relate in exactly the same way to everyone we meet! Such a course of action, if taken to its logical conclusion, would soon result in our being put away! You can easily understand the point if you imagine yourself greeting the assistant who serves you in a large supermarket in the same way as you greet your husband or wife. Try it, and you'll soon have trouble, either in the shop or at home!

Keeping and discarding (3:6-7)

In the realm of material possessions the Preacher warns us of two opposite dangers. On the one hand there is the danger that we breathe the atmosphere of our 'disposable society' too deeply and throw things away too cheaply. That approach to possessions may sound very spiritual. 'They are only things, they don't matter.' But it can mask some very unspiritual motives. It may mask the fact that we are really just trying to keep up with the Joneses and really just want the latest thing to replace the old thing for reasons of status. It may mask an unfeeling attitude to those in need in our world. It may mask very poor stewardship. Such people need to hear that 'there is a time to search..., to keep..., to mend'.

So is it more spiritual to hold on to everything, always patch things up and make do? Not necessarily. That may hide a possessive attitude which invests too much significance in things. The real evidence that God was at work in the life of Zacchaeus was that he was prepared to give his money away! The hoarding mentality may sometimes indicate that we are not travelling lightly enough in this world. It's no mark of spirituality for the ceiling to cave in under the pressure of all that has been stored up in the loft in case it comes in useful one day. Another danger of this approach might be that it does not sufficiently permit enjoyment of God's creation – some of our modern gadgets free us to benefit in this way.

Discernment is needed. It is appropriate at times to keep, protect, preserve and to refuse to replace material possessions. At other times it is equally right to dispose of them. God's direction can be seen in both responses at different times.

Active and passive, positive and negative (3:7-8)

The Preacher sums up by saying that the wise person knows when one form of relationship is called for and when another is more appropriate. It is not always a virtue to call a spade a spade for there are times when it is more constructive to say nothing. Similarly there are times when positive and friendly relations are appropriate with people and times when unfriendly relationships are in order.

Two overall lessons emerge from this passage. First, we need to recognize the divine control which is exercised over our lives. In Psalm 31:15 David, who is clearly facing trouble, expresses his confidence in God like this: 'My times are in your hands.' When we learn to trust God like that it takes away the fretfulness, anxiety and restlessness and leaves us much better able to cope with our situation. He may arrange our diaries differently from the way we would have chosen to fill them. But, so what? He knows best.

That same message is movingly portrayed in the book of Esther. Although it does not even mention God once, it is a powerful witness to his ability to look after things. Esther was a Jewish girl who became queen to King Xerxes just at the time when a holocaust on the Jews was about to be unleashed. Because of her position she was able to persuade the king that he had been unwittingly manipulated by his advisors and the threat against the Jews was removed. Esther's uncle said to her, 'Who knows but that you have come to royal position for such a time as this?' (Esth. 4:14). Although they may not have explicitly mentioned it, they too recognized the providence of God.

The second lesson to emerge from Esther has to do with the human side of things. For all their belief in God's providence, Esther still had to speak and seize the opportunity presented to her. The important thing, says the Preacher, is to understand the time and behave appropriately. The fool misunderstands the time. There is a right moment for things. As Ecclesiastes 8:5 puts it, 'the wise heart will know the proper time and procedure.' Some of David's men, the men of Issachar, were commended as those 'who understood the times and knew what Israel should do' (1 Chr. 12:32). The wise person seeks to imitate them.

Too often we suffer because people lack such wisdom and discernment. It happens on a personal level. Some people don't know when to shut up. Others tell jokes at inappropriate moments. We also suffer in the church. The church is so often inward-looking and preoccupied with its own affairs that it is ignorant about the real world and when she speaks she is not heard because she speaks to a world that does not exist.

With divine providence and human responsibility in partnership we are encouraged to see the passing of time not as a tyranny but as a blessing. Or is it?

Time – Prose and Practicalities (3:9-22)
The first part of the chapter might be great poetry but it's easy to see why some might regard it as a little short on reality. Mr Preacher begins to struggle with the thoughts which intrude from the real world. There life often seems much more like 'doing time' or 'serving time' rather than anything else. The Preacher's mood changes as he starts to argue with himself.

He doesn't give in easily to the negative views that assert themselves and each time an objection is raised he counters it with a thought that brings God into the picture. He is saved from descending into complete scepticism, but in the end he is much more ambivalent, and perhaps much more realistic, about time than he was to start with.

He raises six points for discussion.

Life is a burden (3:9-11)
He returns to familiar territory. It is all very well to have this rose-coloured view of time, but where does it get you in the

end? For the average person life is not like a romantic film from Hollywood; it's a burden.

Where does time get you? Not, he protests, to where you want to go. People never seem to reach the rest, fulfilment and reward for which they are searching. They set off with high hopes, dreams and ambitions as to what they want to achieve by the time they are twenty, or thirty, or forty. But then they find that they are forty-five and they haven't made it! They are climbing the career ladder and have their eyes set on the heights they want to reach. But then, one day, they wake up and it dawns on them that they've been passed over for promotion and they aren't going to realize the dreams they had.

In a worse position still is the person who does achieve all that he has set his heart on, but once there he finds it empty. He's like a child who desperately wants to play with a toy, simply because his sister is playing with it; but once he's got it in his possession he loses all interest in it. It's an empty achievement.

The Preacher begins to shout out at God, 'It's not fair.' He holds God responsible for the situation. He must be some cruel cosmic sadist to inflict such an unenjoyable existence on people.

But when he thinks it through he realizes that maybe God has a reason for laying a burden on human beings. We know from experience that it is uncharacteristic of God to be cruel, for 'he has made everything beautiful in its time' (*verse 11*). Nature and creation teach us that. So why is our experience of life so disappointing?

The Preacher concludes that it is because he has 'set eternity in the hearts of men; yet they cannot fathom what God has done from beginning to end' (*verse 11*). What does that conundrum mean? Simply this: man is not God, so many mysteries and unanswered questions will remain. It is pointless to think that we, as mere human beings, shall ever answer them all. Don't try to play at being God. And yet we are made in the image of God. He is eternal (Ps. 90:2), and that image is deeply implanted within us. So we shall never find fulfilment except in a relationship with him. All other routes to enjoyment will ultimately leave us restless and unsatisfied.

God is eternal, vast, infinite and without beginning or end. We are finite, tiny, flimsy and puny. Yet there is within us all an eternal ache which we long to satisfy. God has put it there. This capacity to plug into eternal things, this deep-down feeling that we must transcend our finite situation, this awareness that the current order of things is not all there is; all these have their origin in God. So we are condemned to want to overcome our immediate situation. We know that there is something more than life on the horizontal offers us. We have a God-given appetite which life under the sun can never fill.

In C.S. Lewis' words:

> God made us; invented us as a man invents an engine. A car is made to run on petrol, and it would not run properly on anything else. Now God designed the human machine to run on himself. He is the fuel our spirits were designed to burn, or the food our spirits were designed to feed on. There is no other.[1]

So if life is a burden, it is simply that God has withheld our ability to enjoy it until we find him, the source of all fulfilment. In the ancient words of Augustine, 'You have made us for yourself, and our hearts are restless until they find their rest in you.'

Contentment is elusive (3:12-13)

Mr Preacher pursues the matter further. He takes eating, drinking and work as three fundamental symbols for where people ought to find satisfaction. Life becomes bearable, from any viewpoint, if we are content with our food, our drink and our work. At the lowest level a person can get by on that even if he never has satisfaction on a higher existential place.

But even here there is a problem. Contentment even at that elementary level is elusive. One person enjoys eating while to another it's a tasteless chore from which he derives no pleasure. Another enjoys drinking and finds every glass or cup as refreshing as a long cool drink on a hot summer's day after some strenuous work in the garden. But to another every drink is like poison and he only downs the brew, of whatever description, because it is a biological necessity. And as for work, job satisfaction is notoriously elusive. Industrialists spend millions every year in research and development in the hope that the workforce will become more contented and therefore more productive. Perhaps, Mr Preacher, is not so simple after all.

It's a curious fact that two people can eat the same meal and one will love it and the other will hate it. Two people can do identical jobs in identical conditions and one will derive satisfaction from it while the other will not. The fault cannot lie in the food, or the drink, or the job, since they are the same. The difference must lie in us. What is the secret of contentment?

The secret is that contentment is a gift from God. One person has it and another does not. The difference lies in whether people have opened up their lives to receive his gift or whether they are struggling through, determined to make it on their own. If it's the latter, contentment will remain elusive.

Earth is unreliable (3:14)

Behind this verse celebrating the enduring nature of God is an unspoken moan. He might endure but nothing else seems to. Everything else about us seems so transitory and unsettled and changeable. Many suffer from what Alvin Toffler defined as 'future shock', which he described as 'the dizzying disorientation brought on by the premature arrival of the future'. He spoke of a 'suspicion that change is out of control'. We look back with longing to a world which seemed much more stable than it is now. C.P. Snow has commented that 'until this century change was so slow that it would pass unnoticed in a person's lifetime. That is no longer so. The rate of change has increased so much that our imagination can't keep up.'[2]

We are helpless passengers of time which is accelerating and driving off wildly into the future, we know not where. Everything around us changes. We even say, 'You know, you are not the man or woman I married five years ago.' So how can we be sure of anything?

Mr Preacher argues the other side of reality. Look at God and you will find a firm footing in the unsteady state of this world. Four claims are made of him and his work.

First, *he is permanent.* 'Everything God does will endure for ever.' He's not like the old 78 record which has been replaced by the LP only in turn to be superseded by the cassette and then the compact disc. He is ever our contemporary and never to be superseded.

Secondly, *he is complete.* 'Nothing can be added to it.' There are no gaps and no inadequacies in God's work. He is not like the computer you bought yesterday, only to wish you had waited till today when a better one is on the market which is capable of a greater range of operations.

Thirdly, *he is secure.* 'Nothing taken from it.' What God does cannot have anything subtracted from it. It cannot be stolen or broken. Its not like investing in unit trusts where you might gain or you might lose. He's secure.

Fourthly, *he is worthy*. 'God does it, so men will revere him.' The Preacher is not saying that God is on some ego-trip and has a need to be worshipped. Rather the whole point of what he is saying is that it is only as we revere God that we ourselves find completion. So God is kind in showing us his work since it is an incentive for us to worship him.

Achievement is futile (3:15)

The doubts about time continue to assail the Preacher's mind. Now it is the thought that 'whatever is has already been, and what will be has been before'. History has no point, no direction. It is useless talking about development or progress. We are caught in an endless cycle from which there is no escape.

The barrister and playwright, John Mortimer, seems to share that opinion. In *Paradise Postponed*, which has been called a long case history of England since 1945, Simeon Simcox says to his wife, just after the Falklands war, 'What we're doing is going round in circles. I mean, is this where we came in?'[3] Forty years had elapsed but nothing had really changed in all that time. It's just the same old story.

But the faith of the Preacher protests that he has misunderstood. 'God will call the past to account.' Behind the apparently ceaseless round of history there is one who is sovereign. As judge he will hold us accountable for the way in which we have lived. But that is just the tip of the iceberg as far as his sovereignty goes. If he is sovereign then history is not a boomerang, always destined to return to its start-point. Rather, events are unfolding according to his plan and working towards a point of consummation. The end is coming when things will change, and change drastically. We cannot say 'this is it'.

Times are evil (3:16-17)
The Preacher instinctively reacts as we all might. If God is going to judge the world, why doesn't he get on with it? Evil seems to have the upper hand. Wherever you look it seems to be in control. Wrong always seems to triumph. Bad people get away with murder while good people suffer. Read any newspaper headline, any day of the week, and you'll know that's true. From Bosnia to Belfast, from Romania to Ruanda, the story is the same. If there is any justice, then it's not to be seen among governments, or the establishment, or the powerful. So why doesn't God step in and do something?

How does the Preacher answer himself this time? By saying that it all depends on your perspective. Look at it this way. There is an old story about a farmer who challenged God and took on his religious neighbours at the same time by doing all his work on Sunday. He got a bumper harvest that year and wrote to the local newspaper saying that he had proved there was no value in Sabbath observance. 'I have been conducting an experiment with one of my fields. I have ploughed it on a Sunday. I sowed the seed on a Sunday. I irrigated and tended it on a Sunday and I reaped it on a Sunday. And I want to tell you that this is the biggest crop in the whole neighbourhood.' The editor of the newspaper simply added a comment, 'God does not settle his accounts in October.'[4]

God doesn't always work to our time scale. 'With the Lord a day is like a thousand years, and a thousand years are like a day' (2 Pet. 3:8). But judgment is assured at some stage in the future. Because it has not happened yet it does not mean it is any less sure. The day is coming when right will triumph and evil will be judged. But it may not be just yet.

Superiority is illusory (3:18-21)
The Preacher's last dialogue with himself is bit obscure. Perhaps the previous thought on the dominance of evil

provides him with a springboard to this one. From the way man behaves it looks as if he is no better than the animals. In fact, perhaps that is unfair to some of the animals! for human beings can be more beastly than many of them would ever dream of.

The idea that man is no more than a 'naked ape' then seems to grow in his mind. Man not only behaves like the animals but breathes the same air as they do (*verse 19*), is made of the same stuff as they are (*verse 20*) and shares the same destiny as they do (*verses 19-20*). (The thought of time, here in the sense of man's future destiny, is with him from the start to finish in this chapter.) So what's the advantage in being human and why do we seem to think that human beings are superior?

It would let us off the hook if we believed that we and the animals were the same. We could live as irresponsibly as a cat if we wanted to. We could wake up in the morning and then spend the rest of the day stretching in the sun, lounging around, playing with someone else's wool, miaouwing for our food or skirmishing with friends. No responsibilities. No worries. Or we could live like a dog. Perhaps barking and biting come easily to us, so why not indulge what comes naturally? Perhaps you feel a different animal would fit you better.

The moment we speak like this we know it's not true. For all his cynicism, the Preacher cannot quite dismiss the thought that man is different. He's left with the puzzling thought as to why God tests man (*verse 18*). He's also left with the uncertainty as to whether life after death is not different for human beings from that experienced by animals (*verse 21*).

He seems to be saying (though the Hebrew is difficult) that without God and without different futures, human beings might just as well be animals. But with God man is more than a naked ape and his future beyond the grave puts him in a different class altogether.

Elsewhere the Bible teaches us that man is unique and that his superiority is not an illusion (Gen. 1:27-31; 2:15-24). He may breathe the same air as the animals and be created from the same stuff but he is a living soul, responsible and accountable and with a different end in view.

In the end, it's all a matter of perspective. There is no question that the Sears Tower is the tallest building in Chicago. Not only is it a measurable fact but, from a distance, it is easy to see its tower stretching above all other buildings around. But I have stood on the pavement outside it and looked up and could have sworn that it was dwarfed by other buildings! It all depends on your perspective.

So it is with time. You can stand and view it from the perspective of the sceptic and unbeliever. It will often seem then as if you are doing time more than anything else. The poetry of the first half of this chapter might move you aesthetically but it will leave you unmoved spiritually. You will know nothing of the providence of your heavenly Father. You will complain that life is a burden; contentment is elusive; earth is unreliable; achievement is futile; times are evil and man's superiority is an illusion.

Or you might stand with the believers and then you will see things very differently. The poetry will lead you to appreciate the providence of God. Time will be coupled with the perspective of eternity. And instead of the complaints there will be the quiet affirmations that God sometimes withholds enjoyment so that we can find our true centre in him; that God gives contentment to all who ask; that God endures unchanging on; that God remembers all our deeds and gives them significance; that God judges all people and their actions in his own good time, and that God tests us that we may realize we are the summit of his creation and very special to him.

If the latter is your perspective, then eat, drink and enjoy your work. Life is not a burden but a blessing under the care of a loving and generous heavenly Father.

References
1. C.S. Lewis, *Mere Christianity* (Fontana, 1952), p. 50.
2. Alvin Toffler, *Future Shock* (Pan Books, 1970), pp. 19, 27, 30.
3. John Mortimer, *Paradise Postponed* (Penguin, 1986), p. 375.
4. John Blanchard, *Not Hearers Only*, vol. 4 (Word, 1974), p.19.

4

ALL THE LONELY PEOPLE
4:1-16

Again I looked and saw all the oppression that was taking place under the sun:

I saw the tears of the oppressed –
    and they have no comforter;
power was on the side of their oppressors –
    and they have no comforter.
[2]And I declared that the dead,
    who had already died,
are happier than the living,
    who are still alive.
[3]But better than both
    is he who has not yet been,
who has not seen the evil
    that is done under the sun.

[4]And I saw that all labour and all achievement spring from man's envy of his neighbour. This too is meaningless, a chasing after the wind.

[5]The fool folds his hands
    and ruins himself.
[6]Better one handful with tranquillity
    than two handfuls with toil
    and chasing after the wind.

[7]Again I saw something meaningless under the sun:

[8]There was a man all alone;
    he had neither son nor brother.
There was no end to his toil,
    yet his eyes were not content with his wealth.
"For whom am I toiling," he asked,
    "and why am I depriving myself of enjoyment?"

59

This too is meaningless –
    a miserable business!

[9]Two are better than one,
    because they have a good return for their work:
[10]If one falls down,
    his friend can help him up.
But pity the man who falls
    and has no-one to help him up!
[11]Also, if two lie down together, they will keep warm.
    But how can one keep warm alone?
[12]Though one may be overpowered,
    two can defend themselves.
A cord of three strands is not quickly broken.

[13]Better a poor but wise youth than an old but foolish king who no longer knows how to take warning. [14]The youth may have come from prison to the kingship, or he may have been born in poverty within his kingdom. [15]I saw that all who lived and walked under the sun followed the youth, the king's successor. [16]There was no end to all the people who were before them. But whose who came later were not pleased with the successor. This too is meaningless, a chasing after the wind.

The Beatles sang about it. One in four people suffers from it. Eleven and a half million people telephone the Samaritans every year as a result of it. One thousand people write to agony aunt Claire Rayner every week because of it. People of all ages suffer from it; children, adolescents, the recently married, the middle-aged and the retired and bereaved. The film *Out of Africa* evocatively portrays the emotions associated with it.

The problem is loneliness.

Once again the Preacher rudely interrupts the smugness of our world and cuts off our escape routes to remind us of the grim reality of life. For one in four that reality is the reality of loneliness.

> All the lonely people
> Where do they all come from?
> All the lonely people
> Where do they all belong?[1]

The Preacher knows that there is more than one cause of loneliness. He introduces four situations in which loneliness is common and in the middle of it all he buries some clues to help people overcome it.

Loneliness caused by oppression (4:1-3)
'I saw the tears of the oppressed – and they have no comforter; power was on the side of their oppressors – and they have no comforter' (*verse 1*). Tyrannical regimes, totalitarian governments and greedy tycoons have a long and dishonourable history of causing whole communities to disintegrate and of breaking up families. Wherever their hand stretches loneliness increases. By their policies and through their violence people are torn apart from each other, taken away from their loved ones and isolated in utter loneliness. For such people the haunting refrain of the preacher, 'they have no comforter', is a nightmare which has become a daytime reality.

The Nazi atrocities of the last war are an outstanding and painful illustration of the Preacher's point. Jews were first herded into ghettos, like animals, and although that brought them into closer contact with each other, the loneliness had already begun. They were cut off from their Gentile neighbours and colleagues. Gradually the isolation increased as radios were confiscated and newspapers were banned. But then came the forced resettlements and the final terror of the concentration camps where even young children were wrenched out of their mother's arms. Loneliness descended as black as a moonless night.

The oppressors still stalk the world. Nowhere is the loneliness of oppression shown more vividly than in the film *The Killing Fields*. It is the story of Dith Pran, a journalist, who was seized by the Khmer Rouge when they took over Cambodia, and was separated from his western colleagues.

The revolutionary forces swept through the land renaming all that came under their control and forcing all the educated people out of the cities to work on the land. Thousands were slaughtered. The bones of the deceased bobbed up and down in well holes like bones in soup. Fields galore grew lush and green where the bodies of those killed had been buried. It's from that observation that the film derives its sad title.

You can almost touch the isolation Dith Pran feels as you watch the film. It's that real. It's especially real when he escapes from the prison chain gangs and begins to make his long solitary way over the border into Thailand. It takes him months of walking through the fields and of hiding from search parties. The most horrific scenes of all are those where he finds himself walking on islands of skeletons, made up of the skulls and bones of those tortured and killed by the Khmer Rouge. In Thailand he finds companionship again. But under the oppressor there was no comforter. That's loneliness.

In the light of this reality the Preacher sees little option but to despair. It would be better, he says, not to have been born than to have to endure this. Verses 2 and 3 are the lowest point in the book. Derek Kidner has commented that there is nothing sadder in the book than this wistful glance at the dead and the unborn.[2] It is a feeling that is commonly shared. Countess von Blixen, the heroine of *Out of Africa,* stands at the graveside of her friend Denys, so tragically killed in a plane crash, and intones:

> Smart lad to slip betimes away,
> From fields where glory does not stay.

The one answer that the Preacher can think of is despair. And yet, that trigger phrase crops up again. He talks of the evil done 'under the sun'. Perhaps he is not quite closing the door on other solutions after all. Perhaps there is more – another perspective which is possible. He doesn't explore it even if there is. He just leaves us with the forcefulness of his bleak conclusion. Without God, surely there is no other solution. Without God, there is no hope. Without God, it is foolish to believe that justice will be done, for in this life it is patently not done. His conclusion, as Michael Eaton has starkly put it, is that 'Godless sorrow leads to suicidal longings'.[3] But he's not about telling us what difference God would make, just yet.

Loneliness caused through competitiveness (4:4-6)

The description of oppression may, mercifully, be very far removed from anything we have experienced. We may be priding ourselves that in the West we know nothing of such loneliness and that our governments give us freedom of movement and association. But beware. If we have escaped the form of loneliness which is endemic to totalitarianism it may only be to fall prey to the form of loneliness endemic to the so-called free West, that is, loneliness caused through competitiveness.

The psychologists tell us how vital the competitive spirit is. It spurs us forward to achieve more than we would ever do without it. It is woven into the very texture of family life and the education system. Its dangers have been recognized there and attempts have been made to minimize its effects, but it cannot be eradicated. The drive is acquired early and runs deep within us. The whole of sport is based on the competitive spirit. The object is to pare a fraction of a second off someone else's record, to climb the league by defeating your opponent, to crush the opposition and win the trophy.

The competitive spirit may have its healthy side. It may be stretching and character-forming. But it quickly degenerates into a self-centred nastiness towards one's fellow competitors.

Michael Argyle, the respected psychologist, rates the need for achievement as next in importance after our biological needs. Having done so he immediately points out the tension to which the Preacher alludes. 'In many social situations,' he writes, 'there is a task to be completed, as in committee work or in research groups. People high in achievement motivations are found to be most concerned with the task, while those in whom affiliative motivation is stronger are more concerned about getting on well with the other group members.'[4] It seems that the competitive spirit inevitably distances one from one's colleagues.

It is in this area of work that the Preacher notices this competitive spirit the most. 'I saw that all labour and all achievement spring from man's envy of his neighbour' (verse 4). It is in the commercial world that competition has its most spiritually debilitating effects. For many industries sheer survival dictates unhealthy competition. It causes us to live in the rat race – which is fine for rats but not for human beings!

It also causes us to set so much store on things which are, in the light of eternity, quite worthless. One of the most interesting magazines I have ever read was the staff magazine for one of the large department stores in Oxford Street. I don't know how anyone can get excited about selling handkerchiefs; but they certainly did. The previous year they were in raptures because the turnover in the handkerchief department at Christmas was up 1%. This year they were in despair because in spite of Miss Blenkinsop's very attractive display she had not achieved the targets of the previous year! I ask you in the light of eternity how is it possible to get so excited about handkerchiefs! The whole emphasis of the magazine was on the ruthless need to sell more, to reach ever higher targets, to increase the turnover. It never seems to have occurred to anyone that maybe we've reached the limit.

We dare not criticize too much because we are all trapped in the same rat race. The thirst for more, the lust for better, the desire to achieve, even if it means trampling on someone else in the process, the drive to be one up, is in us all. Western economic philosophy in general and all recent UK governments, of whatever party, have been founded on the belief that we are competitive individualists. That being so we ought to be aware that it has spiritual consequences as real as those which result from totalitarianism.

The point that Mr Preacher makes is that you cannot live like that without there being personal and social consequences. Personally our spirits become undernourished. We become empty. We end up thinking that life is like chasing the wind. Socially, envy comes between us and our neighbours and cuts us off. We are no longer able to enjoy friendship because either we haven't the time, we are too busy, or we have just stuck a commercial knife in our neighbour's back. Competition destroys relationships and leads to loneliness.

So what's the answer? The temptation is to over-react; to say that if competition and the economic system based on it are so wicked the best thing to do is to drop out. Some have taken just that approach. They do not want to soil their hands with the potential guilt of such a self-centred economic approach, so they have put themselves outside of the system. They don't look for a job, they don't put themselves in the marketplace and they carefully shun the rat race. It comes as something of a shock to hear the Preacher call such people fools and denounce them as on the path to ruin.

In the Preacher's view such an approach is short on reality. You cannot completely absent yourself from the wider system of which you are a part. Those who do so usually draw on the earnings of other people either directly or indirectly. They rely, like it or not, on the system they condemn. But what is worse, they contribute nothing by way of input to that system. Far from helping other people by their actions and overcoming the fragmentation of society, they are themselves behaving in such a way as to cause further breakdown in relationships.

So what is the answer? The Preacher recommends the middle road. On the one hand you refuse to drop out. On the other hand you refuse to get sucked in. You do not catch hold of the competitive spirit with 'two hands' (*verse 6*). You stand back a bit from it. You refuse to be mastered by it. You maintain your objectivity and ability to criticize it. You resist the temptations which are involved, those of envy, greed and indifference to your neighbour. You ensure that there is space in your life for things which nourish the soul and for matter which will be important in eternity. Yet you recognize your wider responsibility and you do your bit. You embrace the need for work with 'one hand' rather than selling out to it with two hands, and thus know peace of mind and spirit.

Loneliness caused by isolation (4:7-8)

Not everyone's loneliness is their own fault. Some are isolated by force of circumstances. They have never married, even if they wanted to do so. Or perhaps they have been widowed early in life without a family around them. It is to this form of loneliness that the Preacher now turns. He draws the picture of a man who desperately wants a companion but none is available. Probably as a result, the man buries himself in work. The trouble is that that only rubs salt in his wounds. He successfully makes money and then realizes that he has no-one to share it with. So what's the point? The sense of loneliness increases.

Work and wealth are no substitutes for love and

companionship. A former Archbishop of Canterbury, Cosmo Lang, was a bachelor. His biographer said of him:

> In the loneliness of his bachelor life his great need was not for friends, of whom he had plenty, any more than work, of which he had too much. It was for that old, simple and human thing – someone in daily nearness to him.[5]

It is possible, of course, to interpret this situation less charitably, and people often do so in a quite unfeeling way and with hurtful consequences for the single person. It is possible to say that this man's toil was not a consequence of his singleness but a cause of it. We could argue that this man had set himself the wrong agenda to begin with; that he was too independent early in life; too concerned to get ahead; too unbending or dominating in his relationships with others; or too shy; or too afraid to risk a relationship in case he was hurt by it, perhaps. Such possibilities need to be faced. Loneliness sometimes does occur because people build up walls around them which others cannot penetrate. But it is not always so. Some are lonely through no fault of their own.

Does the Preacher have anything to say to help such people? Yes. But let's keep his answer until we have explored the final cause of loneliness of which he speaks.

Loneliness caused by power (4:13-16)

The exact meaning of some of these verses is obscure. It's not clear at times precisely who the Preacher is talking about – whether it is the king or the youth – or what their relationship is. Never mind. The overall message is not at all unclear. In a sentence the Preacher says, 'It's lonely at the top, desperately lonely.'

One interpretation of these verses goes like this. An old king isolated himself. He'd been in power so long that he had become stubborn and independent and no longer listened to his advisors (*verse 13*). His self-made loneliness was aggravated by the growing popularity of a young rival. People turned to acknowledge him as their leader. The youth's story was a classic. He'd risen from log cabin to the White House. His humble origins added to the mystique of his power (*verse 14*). He reached the pinnacle of his success (*verse 15*). But then he too suffered from the fatal flaw. His popularity passed, he fell from favour, he became as lonely as the old man he had toppled. So his life too was nothing more than a meaningless wisp of vapour (*verse 16*).

Everyone in high office knows it's lonely at the top. The head teacher, the chief superintendent, the managing director, the Cabinet Minister, the royal prince ... they all have to walk that difficult tightrope between not appearing too aloof unless they lose support and yet maintaining their distance and not becoming one of the crowd. From a distance their diaries look full of exciting meaningful activity. But those who've been there know that their lives are just as empty and lonely as those of others.

A major factor in causing the isolation is the fact that the responsibility stops with the person at the top. The 'buck stops here' syndrome makes a difference. In the end others can excuse themselves, leave, resign, pretend they didn't decide, get out in a multitude of acceptable ways. But not the person at the top. Was it Lyndon B. Johnson who said that the loneliest moment that anyone could experience was when the phone rang in the middle of the night and woke you from sleep and a voice said, 'Mr President, I have a call for you'; and then there was a split second before you were connected? That split second felt like an eternity. What had happened? Why were you being wakened? Had a nuclear accident taken place? Had some mistake occurred and war begun? What major tragedy was about to be reported? Then the full weight and the full loneliness of office fell upon a mortal human being's shoulders – and it hurt.

But ultimately, it's not the responsibility of office that Mr Preacher is concerned with. Ultimately, it is the fickleness of people. One moment you're a popular public figure. The next you're a nobody... deserted by all your former supporters. Churchill knew that after the Second World War. Khrushchev knew it from 1964 onwards.

Jimmy Carter faced it with his usual disarming honesty. In 1984, when Ronald Reagan and Walter Mondale fought each other for the US Presidency, the press went looking for ex-President Carter. Why wasn't he on the campaign trail supporting his party's nominee? Eventually they tracked him down to the burnt-out ruins of 742 East Sixth Street, Lower East Side, New York. Amid rotting floorboards and sagging ceilings Jimmy Carter, with carpenter's tools in hand, was restoring the building to a habitable condition to provide low-cost housing for the poor. The questions poured out. Wouldn't he rather be involved in politics? Wasn't it odd for the former President to be doing this? One asked, 'What does it feel like for a former President to become a carpenter?' Jimmy Carter smiled and simply replied, 'That's how fleeting fame is.' The Preacher in Ecclesiastes would have agreed with him.

Many a football-team manager has had the same experience. While success comes his way everything is fine. But if the team plummets in the division then they are soon on the way out. There's little mercy either in the Board room or among the spectators.

The scenario of power, says the Preacher, is a great anticlimax. You work to achieve fame and influence and once you've got it, then.... nothing, emptiness, loneliness. All life is contaminated by loneliness and no position in life is exempt from its grasp.

Loneliness: is there an answer? (4:9-13)

The Preacher's sorry, but far from complete, catalogue of the sources of loneliness causes even the most sociable of spirits to feel somewhat depressed. It's all very well to 'tell it like it is', but doesn't the Preacher have some responsibility to give us hope? Surely it's destructive and irresponsible just to recount the dark side?

In fairness, the Preacher does give two clues as to how loneliness can be overcome. He doesn't develop them into techniques and therapies as we would want him to do today. But at least he sets us on the right road. First he points to the value of human companionship (*verses 9-12*), and secondly, he points to the value of true wisdom (*verse 13*).

The value of human companionship (4:9-12)

With sublime simplicity he reminds us that 'two are better than one'. Many a romantic sermon has been preached at wedding services on the basis of these verses! They are understandable since marriage would seem to be the ultimate illustration of what he is saying. But whether the Preacher had marriage in mind is doubtful, since that would make the third person, mentioned in verse 12, a gooseberry. Two's company but three's a crowd. Furthermore, to apply these verses exclusively to marriage would condemn many single people to a lifetime of loneliness.

We must insist that the Preacher is talking more widely. He probably has in mind the idea, common enough in his day, of having to make a journey at night. It is then self-evident that two are better than one. Charles Swindoll summarizes the advantages of a companion is such circumstances. A companion provides:

> Mutual encouragement when we are weak,
> Mutual support when we are vulnerable,
> Mutual protection when we are attacked.[6]

You only have to think of the plight of old people living on their own during a cold spell to know the truth of his words. What a difference it makes to have someone to share such days with. How it eases the burdens and provides confidence and hope. To this self-evident dictum the Preacher adds the line, 'a cord of three strands is not quickly broken'. Marriage sermons say that this is where God comes in! Intimate human companionship in marriage is great, but to have God interwoven into the relationship between husband and wife is greater still. It's a nice thought and a true one. But I doubt that it is the one the original Preacher had in mind! He does not appear suddenly to be opening up a vertical shaft of light into an otherwise dark horizontal picture. Rather he seems simply to be making use of a common enough saying that a three-stranded rope is hard to break; much harder than a single strand.

In other words there is nothing special in this context about a twofold relationship. A small group of three, or even four, will have the same effect. It's human companionship that we need. For many it includes marriage. For others, who do not have that relationship, rich companionship can still be found in a small group of friends.

There will, of course, be differences between the marriage relationship and the friendship relationship. The sexual intercourse element of marriage must be lacking in the wider group. The friendship relationship dare not be exclusive or it will be destructive and will exclude potential marriage partners who could provide more intimate companionship. Margaret Evening, who has written most sensitively as a single person, quotes C.S. Lewis as characterizing the difference like this; 'Lovers are normally face to face; friends side by side, absorbed in some common interest.'[7] Many a wholesome and pure relationship between friends has helped to banish loneliness and provide enrichment for single people.

Of course, wisdom needs to be exercised. It would be foolish to pretend that close relationships between single people and married couples have not led to love tangles: the problem of the eternal triangle. Care needs to be exercised. Moreover close relationships between individual friends of the same or opposite sex need to be watched today so that some of the pitfalls are avoided. The pity is that the dirty minds of the generation in which we live often suspect such relationships, quite wrongly. Christians should wisely resist such pressures and show that healthy companionship can be enjoyed as God intended.

In a nutshell, the Preacher is saying that if you find yourself lonely God invites you to do something about it. John Milton said that the first thing God pronounced 'not good' was the loneliness of man. Until that time everything that God had made he pronounced to be good. God did not make you to be lonely. He made you for companionship.

So, with confidence, take steps to find yourself companionship. The steps you need to take may be very practical. Some people live in a single-sex environment or worship in an almost single-sex church. Create opportunities where you will meet eligible partners! Some are shy and need to be taught social skills and to be encouraged to grow in self-confidence. Some need to take the initiative in reaching out to others rather than waiting for others to reach out to them, and complaining when they don't. People can offer hospitality in the humblest of circumstances. Living in a bed-sitter doesn't condemn you to be always on the receiving end of hospitality.

Often the blockage is in the mind. Many fail to make friends because they have already decided that no-one will want to be their friend. Others destroy any blossoming friendship because they become too possessive or too dominant or too inflexible. A relationship must be give-and-take. Some find it hard to give and foist all their demands on a partner who quickly realizes that he or she will not be able to cope. But others find it hard to take. Some have never learned to accept love, or help, or gifts. Companionship demands that we do both.

Loneliness should be banished from the Christian church. We ought to be able to express our needs and weaknesses to one another there. In the church we ought to be able to find the help we need to grow and change and mature as persons. We ought also to be able to find the love, friendship and patience there that all of us need. Such needs are not the result of psychological inadequacy. We need not feel guilty about them. They are expressions of the way God made us.

The value of divine wisdom (4:13)
The Preacher's second answer is no more than a clue. It would be easy to miss it. But there's value in noting it and chasing it through to a conclusion. In verse 13 he points to something of importance beyond the human level of making friends. You may have many a friend but still be lonely.

Look again at the picture he draws in verse 13. There are two people in it. One is old, rich and powerful. The other is young and poor. We would naturally think that the former had all the advantages. Certainly the Old Testament would naturally credit him with respect because of his age and assume that he would be wise since he would have been schooled by life's experience. But that's the startling thing. This old man is bereft of wisdom and it's the youth who is said to be wise.

Experience is not an automatic teacher. Job recognized that old people may lose the wisdom they had accumulated over the years (Job 12:20). It needs to be pursued avidly, and once obtained to be guarded jealously.

So just what is wisdom? 'The fear of the LORD is the beginning of wisdom' (Prov. 9:10).

The questions of loneliness is sometimes not a question about our situation at all; it's a question about us. We can see two people in identical situations which, on the surface, seem quite isolating, and one person will be very lonely and the other will be quite content. Or we can take two people in identical situations which seem equally full of companions, and one person will be happily fulfilled and the other full of moans that he or she is lonely. The difference lies in the person – not the situation.

There is no way to overcome loneliness except by wisdom. Without that we can be surrounded by friends and still experience the aching void of existential aloneness. But wisdom leads us into a relationship with God and that relationship means that we can stand without any human companion in the universe and be in touch with our Creator and know that we'll never walk alone.

Listen to the testimony of Armando Valladares, a man who was held prisoner in Fidel Castro's gaol on suspicion of counter-revolutionary activity, who witnessed the most terrifying brutality and who did not know what his own fate would be. In his prison diaries he writes about his early days in confinement.

There were nights when there would be ten or twelve executions. You would hear the bars of the men's cell and cry to him a last goodbye. There was no way to sleep in the *galeras*. That was when God began to become a constant companion of mine and when death became a door into true life, a step from the shadows into eternal light.[8]

When you're down and out,
when you're on the street,
when evening falls so hard,

> I'll comfort you.
> I'll take your part
> Oh, when darkness comes
> and pain is all around
> like a bridge over troubled water
> I will lay me down.[9]

Jesus is the bridge over the troubled waters of loneliness who laid down his life for us. He is the one who promises, 'Never will I leave you, never will I forsake you' (Heb. 13:5). And he's true to his word. Wisdom leads you to him, and then as we learn from him and obey him at a practical level, the loneliness begins to evaporate.

References
1. Lennon and McCartney, 'Eleanor Rigby'.
2. Derek Kidner, *The Message of Ecclesiastes* (IVP, 1976), p. 44.
3. Michael Eaton, *Ecclesiastes* (Tyndale Old Testament Commentaries, IVP, 1983), p.92.
4. Michael Argyle, *The Psychology of Interpersonal Behaviour* (Penguin, 1972), p. 24.
5. J.G. Lockhart, *Cosmo Gordon Lang* (Hodder & Stoughton, 1949).
6. Charles Swindoll, *Living on the Ragged Edge* (Word, 1986), p. 134.
7. Margaret Evening, *Who Walk Alone* (Hodder & Stoughton, 1974), p. 43.
8. Armando Valladares, *Prison Memoirs* (Hamish Hamilton, 1986), p. 32.
9. Paul Simon, 'Bridge over troubled water.'

5

STAND IN AWE
5:1-7

[1]Guard your steps when you go to the house of God. Go near to listen rather than to offer the sacrifice of fools, who do not know that they do wrong.

[2]Do not be quick with your mouth,
 do not be hasty in your heart
 to utter anything before God.
God is in heaven
 and you are on earth,
 so let your words be few.
 [3] As a dream comes when there are many cares,
 so the speech of a fool when there are many words.

[4]When you make a vow to God, do not delay in fulfilling it. He has no pleasure in fools; fulfil your vow. [5]It is better not to vow than to make a vow and not fulfil it. [6]Do not let your mouth lead you into sin. And do not protest to the temple messenger, "My vow was a mistake." Why should God be angry at what you say and destroy the work of your hands? [7]Much dreaming and many words are meaningless. Therefore stand in awe of God.

A guest at a Cambridge college was taken aback one evening when invited to say grace before dinner. He knew no graces and even less Latin, the language in which, since this was Cambridge, the grace would need to be said. But with great mental agility, and even greater temerity, he stood and intoned, 'Omo, Lux, Domestos, Brobat, Ajax, Amen.' The assembled company solemnly said 'Amen' and sat down to eat. No-one had noticed the absurdity of what he said.

Sometimes our worship is just as meaningless.

When we worship we feel the compulsion to say something.

We feel we have to fill the moments with words and we are embarrassed by silence. But this urge for noise betrays us. It shows that we have not really understood what worship is all about.

There have been more disputes in recent days about worship than about almost anything else in the church. The easiest way to divide a church is to introduce change into the inherited patterns of worship. New music, new orders of service, new forms of prayer alike are greeted by many with suspicion and protest. They feel threatened when the old and familiar begins to disappear. On the other side, however, there are equally people for whom those old forms can't disappear fast enough. As far as they are concerned, the sooner tradition is overthrown and novelty and spontaneity are introduced the better. But while we side with one view or the other we reveal our ignorance: we haven't the foggiest clue what worship really is.

C.S. Lewis wrote:

As long as you notice and have to count the steps, you are not yet dancing, but only learning to dance. A good shoe is a shoe you don't notice. Good reading becomes possible when you need not consciously think about eyes, or light, or print, or spelling. The perfect church service would be one we were most unaware of; our attention would have been on God.[1]

He has hit the nail on the head. While we are conscious in our worship of the external, and complain because the flowers are poorly displayed, or because they are singing that awful chorus again, or because you have to endure that traditional anthem, or because it's a hymn-prayer sandwich again or because they've used drama in the sanctuary, or because the vicar isn't wearing robes and so on, we have not begun to worship.

So let's go deeper and see if *we* can learn.

Ecclesiastes 5:1-7 comes as something of a shock to us. The Preacher's concern until now has been with the reality of the world outside the church. Now he steps into church to see what's going on there. The world has left him in despair. Is the church going to fare any better? One thing is sure, he will speak as he finds. We can expect some vigorous criticism. And we are not disappointed.

Our approach before worship (5:1)
'Guard your steps when you go to the house of the God. Go near to listen rather than to offer the sacrifice of fools, who do not know that they do wrong.'

As the Preacher wrote those words he would have had Solomon's temple in his mind's eye. He would have pictured the thousands streaming up to that magnificent building every day to offer sacrifice and worship. It was an immense building, one of the amazing sights of the ancient world, lavishly decorated and awe-inspiring. It dwarfed the worshipper. But that was deliberate, for in making the worshipper feel small it encouraged him to look heavenwards to almighty God. It would strike a responsive cord of humility and wonder in all but the hardest of cynics or the most familiar of its patrons.

It is no longer so popular today to build grand temples and cathedrals as visual aids which point people beyond themselves, although our skylines are still dominated by the church buildings of yesteryear. No matter, for the house of God does not have to be an impressive building. It may be a grand cathedral or a tin hut or even a private bedroom. The 'house of God' is simply that place where God lives, where he can be found and where we can communicate with him. Certain types of buildings may help but they are far from essential. God cannot be limited to them (1 Kgs. 8:27).

Worship is about entering the presence of almighty God.

It is communicating with him. When we understand that, we also understand why the Preacher give terse, straight-from-the-shoulder advice as to how we are to approach worship. In effect he says, 'Watch it!' If we are going to enter the presence of one who is so great, so holy, so awesome, so majestic and powerful, we are about to put ourselves in the danger zone. We dare not do so casually or lightly. We would not dream of being casual in a nuclear reactor plant so why be casual in the presence of the one who designed and invented nuclear energy from nothing in the first place?

When we enter church for another service, do we sense that God is going to be there in living communication with his people?

For eight years, while I lectured at a Bible college, I travelled the country most weekends preaching in different churches. I could easily divide those churches into two distinct camps. On one hand there were those for whom Sunday worship was clearly no more than a habit, a ritual, a social event, a routine activity because, well ... that's what you did on Sunday. They came, they sat through, they went. They had done their bit for God. They had done their duty. It made little difference to them although they may have gone home with a nice warm glow inside. It was just that it was the done thing.

On the other hand there were those churches where I was immediately conscious of a different atmosphere. As you entered the sanctuary it was evident that these people were expecting to meet with God. They were anticipating his presence and looking to him to speak, to do something among them and to change lives.

Their attention was not focused on one another but on him.

Our worship often reminds me of a birthday party where all the guests are so busy exchanging presents with one another that the birthday boy or girl is totally ignored. So much of our worship is taken up with relations with each other and feelings about each other that God gets squeezed out. We go to church because we must see Mrs Carruthers about the coffee morning, or Mr Postlethwaite about the church roof, or Miss Carter-Snare because she's attractive and you really want to invite her out. Or we go determined to avoid certain people. So we make sure we sit on the opposite side from Mrs Ponsonby because she is supposed to have said something rude about us this week which we have picked up fifth-hand, or we get out quick at the end of the service to avoid having to talk to Mr Smith because we can't stand the man! And that's worship?

Jim Graham has written:

> Often the times when we come together as Christians are characterized by good humour, affability, camaraderie, zeal, high spirits (all in themselves pleasant and commendable enough); hardly ever do we find gatherings which are unmistakably characterized by the over-shadowing of the presence of God.[2]

The Preacher says worship may be dangerous, so 'Watch it!' He implies that we should prepare ourselves to enter the temple. Not many people need convincing to prepare their external appearance to go to worship. Most wash themselves and comb their hair before they come. Most turn out their Sunday best, their hat, or their designer labelled clothes, according to their generation and sex. But what about their inner preparation? Do they pray, tune in their hearts and minds to the spiritual wavelength, confess their sin, put their relationships right and raise their level of faith? Jesus said that it was essential for us to do so if our worship was to be acceptable to God (Matt. 5:23-24).

I often hear the complaint that worship is boring. Sometimes it is. A friend of mine was preaching in a church in the north of England where the service, led by the resident team, had been extremely dull. He didn't find in it the inspiration he needed to enable him to preach easily. So before the sermon he knelt at his prayer stool to pray and simply said aloud, 'O Lord, this service has been a crushing bore. I need your help to preach with any power tonight. Amen.' To his acute embarrassment, the microphone in front of him was live and the message was duly delivered not just to the Almighty but to the assembled congregation as well!

Yes, ministers and vicars can find church services dull as well. Sometimes it is their own fault. But I wonder how often it is the fault of those in the pew. What have they contributed? How did they prepare? What were they expecting? What feedback did they give? The fault may equally lie there. Trying to lead some people in worship is like stirring thick treacle or starting a reluctant car engine on a very cold morning. Worship is most boring when people are out of touch with God.

So, when it comes to worship, 'Watch it!' If there is no serious intent on the part of us worshippers to let God communicate with us we are offering 'the sacrifice of fools'. And often, it has to be said, the thought that God might communicate is far from what people expect or want.

Our attitude during worship (5:2-3)

The Preacher continues to develop his theme and to show us the poverty of worship in his day and ours. In this area too we have to say that there is 'nothing new under the sun'. His thinking moves from when we go to worship to what happens when we are at worship. Again his advice is terse. Having told us to 'Watch it!', he now tells us to 'Shut up!' Mercifully the blunt command is followed by a reason and then justified by a fuller explanation.

The command

'Do not be quick with your mouth, do not be hasty in your heart to utter anything before God ... let your words be few.' He knows full well that what most of us do is to come rushing into worship full of ourselves. Mentally and therefore verbally we are the centre of our universe. Our prayers are full of our burdens and concerns, our intercessions and desires, and are voiced in our cant phrases. Our thoughts are full of our pet likes and dislikes, our joys and hates. We filter everything that happens through the sieve of what's pleasing to us, what is entertaining, what is attractive and what is relevant to our small lives.

The fact is that we are so busy talking that God is often quite incapable of getting a word in edgeways. We spend our time trying to get God to agree with us, to adopt our views, to come down on our side, to get God to see things from our viewpoint and to make life comfortable for us.

We have turned worship inside out. True worship means that we bring our puny lives and concerns to God and lay them in surrender at his feet so that we might find out his viewpoint, be instructed by his truth, be directed by his ways and bring our lives into conformity with his will.

Our world is dominated by noise. Words pour forth in their millions from a plethora of TV and radio channels every day. We hear thousands of words daily although we only listen to a fraction of that number. We frequently have a programme on in the background but have to admit, when asked, that we do not know what has just been said. Noise is part of our environment. So it is hard to concentrate and harder still to switch off. But if worship is to be genuine we must learn to cut out the background noise, to stop the chatter, to switch off from ourselves and to tune in and listen to God.

The reason

The Preacher buries the reason for his burden about worship in the middle of his command. We should be careful what we say because 'God is in heaven and you are on earth'. God is God and you are you and there is a world of difference between the two. Soren Kierkegaard spoke about 'the infinite qualitative distinction' between us and God. Exactly.

When you think of it God is almost everything we are not:

> God is infinite, we are finite.
> God is immortal, we are mortal.
> God is invisible, we are visible.
> God is spirit, we are flesh.
> God is almighty, we are weak.
> God is holy, we are sinners.
> God is absolutely pure, we are impure.
> God is omniscient, we are ignorant.
> God is unchangeable, we are fickle.
> God is faithful, we are unfaithful.
> God is loving, we, at best, only know partial love.

So what have we got to teach him of which he is ignorant, and what have we got to fear from him? We have nothing to teach him and everything to learn from him. We have nothing to fear from him and every reason to listen to him that we might trust him more.

By his very nature, God sees the invisible and hears the inaudible. So we cannot fool him with right-sounding words. They may impress our neighbours in church but not God in heaven. As LeRoy Eims perceptively commented, 'We don't pray into a spiritual microphone with God listening on a set of heavenly earphones. He listens to us pray with a spiritual stethoscope.'[3] He hears the unspoken. He hears what is going on in the inside, in the unexpressed desires and ambitions we have. We might put up a good show. But we cannot fool God.

We would do well to learn from some of the great prayers of the Bible. Take Abraham in Genesis 18:23-33, or Solomon in 2 Chronicles 6:12-42, or Nehemiah in Nehemiah 1:4-11, or the early Christians in Acts 4:24-31. Each of these give us the correct pattern for prayer. The element of request is tiny and the basis for it is the character of God. Before the request there is a careful celebration of the character of God. The request is soaked in what God is like. That is why they could pray with such faith and find their prayers were answered. Are we as concerned about God as they were, or is our vision filled to the horizon with ourselves?

The explanation
The Preacher is anxious to explain the matter further. You can, he says, almost measure how big a fool someone is by how many words he uses. The quicker the words tumble out the greater the fool the speaker is likely to be. The Preacher was stating what was commonly accepted by wise teachers of his day. 'The more you talk, the more likely you are to sin. If you are wise, you will keep quiet' (Prov. 10:19, GNB).

Conversely the book of Proverbs, in words which have given great encouragement to anxious tongue-tied students in seminars, teaches that 'even a fool may be thought wise and intelligent if he stays quiet and keeps his mouth shut' (17:27, GNB).

We know how little meaning words have in our world. We make promises only to break them. We spend millions in the law courts every year so that lawyers can argue about what they really mean. Politicians even deliberately cultivate the art of saying a lot and nothing at the same time. Take this quote of Tom King, the former Defence Secretary, who, some years ago, according to the *Sunday Times,* was clarifying the Irish situation in an interview on the *PM* radio programme by making the following definitive statement we'd all been waiting for. He said:

> We believe ... er ... that it should be possible to have discussions ... er ... to see whether it is possible to have talks, but during this ... er ... period, in which we see whether such discussions can be held to see whether there is a basis on which talks can go forward, these talks are being entered into by either side with no precondition ... er ...and ... er ... that is quite clearly understood on either side. We're not talking about talks. We're talking about quite a separate discussion probably conducted at a lower level; exploratory discussion to see if a basis exists on which talks might then be held.

But it's unfair to pick on Tom King. He had a difficult enough job. Every day, examples of gobbledegook abound. The nation seems to run on the basis of obscurity shrouded by words. The words come tumbling out, but are meaningless. And they are sometimes meant to be.

Is there a danger that our worship is the same? The words pour out like water pouring over the Niagara Falls. But our minds and hearts are elsewhere. The Preacher mentions not only words but dreams. Perhaps here he is aware of the daydreaming that goes on while the service of worship proceeds. We respond to the commands of the worship leader to stand and sing the hymn but we cannot tell anyone afterwards what the hymn was because our minds were really back at home sorting out the DIY job or cooking the dinner! We sit through the prayers and the sermons but all the time we're thinking of tomorrow's trip to the supermarket or the task that awaits us at work or the number of light bulbs in the church roof. What we are doing may well be significant to us but it's not worship. It's verbal doodling.[4]

Worship is so much more than words. No better statement

about what it is has ever been framed than that by Archbishop Temple. He wrote:

> Worship is the submission of all of our nature to God. It is the quickening of our consciences by his holiness; the nourishment of our minds with his truth; the purifying of our imagination by his beauty; the opening of the heart to his love; the surrender of will to his purpose – and all gathered up in adoration, the most selfless emotion of which we are capable and therefore the chief remedy for that self-centredness which is our original sin and the source of all actual sin.[5]

Is that our approach to worship? If worship is the highest activity in which people can engage, we should not only come to it with great care but go through it with greater discipline. Our senses should be heightened, our spiritual eyes and ears alert, our minds attentive: for the King is about to address us.

Our actions after worship (5:4-6)

You might by now be wanting to protest. Worship isn't like that for you. You find it a deeply moving experience and would even confess that there are times when you have come to worship with your mind caught up with all sorts of things only gradually to be captivated and to have your thoughts centred on God.

Then, says the preacher, there is another danger to which you might be exposed. And if we are honest, we have all fallen into the trap he is about to unveil. There is the danger that when we are caught up in the emotion of the moment we promise things to God that we later fail to deliver.

We have heard a stirring sermon on missions, so we promise that we will go overseas for God. We have been soundly rebuked about our low level of giving, so we promise God that we will at least begin to tithe. We have been moved by compassion for people's need and we promise God that we will engage in practical Christian service. We have been convicted of our sin and of the way we so easily give in to a particular temptation. We have been challenged about the grudge we have against a fellow Christian so we vow to put it right as soon as the benediction has been pronounced. The music of 'Abba, Father, let me be yours and your alone...', and we have surrendered everything to God.

But the next day it's different. We hedge our missionary commitment about with conditions. We begin to squirm out of our commitment to tithe. We are somehow too busy to get around to that piece of practical Christian service. We face that particular temptation and it looks so attractive that we give in. We make the excuse that we couldn't find our Christian friend after the service to apologize. And, in the ordinary pressures of life, we forget that we are God's and God's alone. The promises we make in haste we repent of at leisure. We say we didn't quite mean it and no-one else heard it and God would understand. But will he?

The Preacher says, 'Come off it!' If you have made a promise to God there are two pieces of advice he has for you.

Don't delay in delivering it (5:4)
It was a vow freely and voluntarily entered into. There was no need to do so but you have. So don't hold back now. The fate of Ananias and Sapphira (Acts 5:1-11) should be sufficient to demonstrate the seriousness of trying to trick God. No pressure had been put on them at all but they had promised to bring all their money to God. Instead they kept some back. There would have been nothing wrong with their doing so if they had not promised otherwise and then lived in pretence.

Don't deny you said it (5:6)

We cannot be sure who the messenger is whom verse 6 mentions. It could be a messenger from the Lord, the messenger of conscience, or more likely, a messenger from the temple. Certainly we can picture the scene. We have given some public indication of our commitment by signing a pledge, sharing our thoughts with someone else or by going forward in response to some appeal. When someone tries to help us follow that commitment through, we begin to deny we ever said it.

The Preacher tries to get us to understand the seriousness of what we have done. We have spoken to the God of heaven whose word is always true and who is constitutionally unable to lie. We cannot lie or pretend to him without offending his nature. He is a holy and righteous God, and one who holds us to account for what we say.

All that we are doing is making ourselves out to be fools. But God, we are told, 'has no pleasure in fools'. That, as Derek Kidner has said, 'is quite as crushing a remark as any in the book'.[6]

Perhaps the Spirit of God is reminding you as you read these words of a promise made long ago which you have never done anything about. Perhaps, in the mercy of God, it is not too late to put it right. Our God is not only a God of holiness but also one of grace, of forgiveness, of restoration and one who makes new beginnings possible.

But no amount of emphasis on his grace can justify us in taking liberties with him or being casual in our worship. We must realise that to worship is to stand in the presence of almighty God and to be in living communication with him. That requires careful preparation before we come, reverent attitudes while we are there and prompt and obedient actions when we leave.

Let me quote again the words of Derek Kidner:

The target for the preacher is the well-meaning person who likes a good sing and turns up cheerfully enough to church, but who listens with half an ear and never gets around quite to what he has volunteered to do for God.[7]

That being so, most of us are in the target zone. But let's not foolishly rush to babble our apologies or gabble our renewed commitments, in case all that we succeed in doing is to compound our sin. Let us rather be silent and stand in awe of God.

References
1. C. S. Lewis, *Letters to Malcolm Chiefly on Prayer* (Geoffrey Bles, 1964), p. 4.
2. Jim Graham, *The Giant Awakes* (Marshall, Morgan & Scott, 1982), pp. 38f.
3. LeRoy Eims, *Be The Leader You Were Meant To Be* (Victor Books, 1975), p.22.
4. Derek Kidner, *The Message of Ecclesiastes* (IVP, 1976), p. 53.
5. William Temple, *Readings in St John's Gospel* (Macmillan, 1968 edn.), p. 68.
6. Kidner, p. 53.
7. *Ibid.*, p. 53.

6

MONEY, MONEY, MONEY!
5:8-6:12

[8]If you see the poor oppressed in a district, and justice and rights denied, do not be surprised at such things; for one official is eyed by a higher one, and over them both are others higher still. [9]The increase from the land is taken by all; the king himself profits from the fields.

[10]Whoever loves money never has money enough;
   whoever loves wealth is never satisfied with his income.
   This too is meaningless.

[11]As goods increase,
   so do those who consume them.
And what benefit are they to the owner
   except to feast his eyes on them?

[12]The sleep of a labourer is sweet,
   whether he eats little or much,
but the abundance of a rich man
   permits him no sleep.

[13]I have seen a grievous evil under the sun:

wealth hoarded to the harm of its owner,
   [14]or wealth lost through some misfortune,
so that when he has a son
   there is nothing left for him.
[15]Naked a man comes from his mother's womb,
   and as he comes, so he departs.
He takes nothing from his labour
   that he can carry in his hand.

[16]This too is a grievous evil:
   As a man comes, so he departs,
      and what does he gain,
      since he toils for the wind?
[17]All his days he eats in darkness,
   with great frustration, affliction and anger.

90

[18]Then I realised that it is good and proper for a man to eat and drink, and to find satisfaction in his toilsome labour under the sun during the few days of life God has given him – for this is his lot. [19]Moreover, when God gives any man wealth and possessions, and enables him to enjoy them, to accept his lot and be happy in his work – this is a gift of God. [20]He seldom reflects on the days of his life, because God keeps him occupied with gladness of heart.

[1]I have seen another evil under the sun, and it weighs heavily on men: [2]God gives man wealth, possessions and honour, so that he lacks nothing his heart desires, but God does not enable him to enjoy them, and a stranger enjoys them instead. This is meaningless, a grievous evil.

[3]A man may have a hundred children and live many years; yet no matter how long he lives, if he cannot enjoy his prosperity and does not receive proper burial, I say that a stillborn child is better off than he. [4]It comes without meaning, it departs in darkness, and in darkness its name is shrouded. [5]Though it never saw the sun or knew anything, it has more rest than does that man – [6]even if he lives a thousand years twice over but fails to enjoy his prosperity. Do not all go to the same place?

[7]All man's efforts are for his mouth,
    yet his appetite is never satisfied.
[8]What advantage has a wise man over a fool?
    What does a poor man gain
    by knowing how to conduct himself before others?
[9]Better what the eye sees
    than the roving of the appetite.
This too is meaningless,
    a chasing after the wind.

[10]Whatever exists has already been named,
    and what man is has been known;
no man can contend
    with one who is stronger than he.
[11]The more the words,
    the less the meaning,
    and how does that profit anyone?

[12]For who knows what is good for a man in life, during the few and meaningless days he passes through like a shadow? Who can tell him what will happen under the sun after he is gone?

Let me invite you to dream. Wouldn't it be wonderful to be really rich! Have you ever thought what it would be like to be a Richard Branson? Still a young man, he's a millionaire several times over, and he employs over two thousand people in 27 different countries. He owns Virgin Atlantic Airways, a railway company, and over one hundred other companies, several of which bear the name of Virgin. He's got sixty-eight record shops and contracts with over two hundred bands.

After naming his record company Virgin he discovered that there was a group of islands called Virgin. So one weekend, on his way back to Europe from the USA, he stopped off to see them, and bought one of them. You can rent it for $5,500 a day if you want to.

Just for pleasure he has a perfect replica of an 1890s Mississippi paddle-steamer, his own executive jet and a one-and-a-half acre roof garden in central London. As icing on the cake he owns a lovely manor house in rural Oxfordshire to which he and his family can retreat at weekends. It makes a nice change from the boathouse where he normally lives during the week.

He likes adventure, and having secured the record for the fastest transatlantic crossing in his *Virgin Atlantic Challenger II*, he is now trying to secure the round the world record.

It must be an exciting life! It's certainly got style!

He's a self-made man. He started his record company in 1970 while he was still a teenager, and by 1997 he was the fifth richest person in the United Kingdom with £1,700 million to his name. He puts down his success to his innocence and love of a challenge.

Carry on dreaming. Just imagine what it would be like to have all that money in the bank, to have all those people to dance attendance on you, to be able to travel wherever you like and do whatever you want. Wouldn't it be great?

The Preacher replies to such questions with a blunt 'No!' Contrary to most dreams and in defiance of popular thought the Preacher insists that money does not make a person happy. When we stop to think about it we know he's right. We only have to think back to the bizarre life of Howard Hughes to know there is no connection between wealth and happiness. But we are slow learners and so the Preacher provides us with a rigorous exposure of what money does.

If you wish you had more, listen to this.

What wealth does (5:8-13)
In the cool light of day, wealth may be said to achieve three things.

It increases your appetite but not your satisfaction (5:10)
Whoever loves money never has enough. Whoever loves wealth is destined to be constantly hungry for more. It's another of those insane enigmas of life. All that the possession of wealth does is to create an insatiable appetite for more. It creates within us a craving desire which is never satisfied. In a famous saying of the late Duchess of Windsor, 'One can never be too rich, or too thin.' One of the Rockafellers, when asked which million he most enjoyed making, replied, 'The next one.'

In the end it becomes your master, dominates your thinking and enslaves you.

It increases your dependants but not your income (5:11)
If you are wealthy you are worth knowing. So people ingratiate themselves with you. They begin to find a way into your circle and angle a way to your parties.

The blatant way in which this fawning takes place was admitted a few years ago in a *Sunday Times Magazine* article by Michael Caine who described the sickly pretence of Hollywood. Hollywood society is extremely stratified and it's clear whom you should invite and whom you should avoid inviting to your parties. It also means people spend a good deal of time dropping hints and trying to secure invitations to the right parties. Most of the conversation is work-oriented and being there is the way to get on. For, he wrote, 'in Hollywood society there is something even more frightening than AIDS, and that's failure. You never mix with anyone who's failed. The failures have their own parties.' Hollywood is full of snobs and nobs and bores ... and Michael Caine has suffered them all.

It's an exact illustration of what the Preacher claims. If you are wealthy you are liable to collect around you a group of hangers-on who contribute absolutely nothing to you, but cost you a lot.

If you were on the dole they wouldn't want to know you.

It increases your insomnia but not your contentment (5:12)
The obvious reason the rich person doesn't sleep is that he is worried about protecting all that money. But these days, with burglar alarms, double locks, safes and banks, maybe that is not the real reason for insomnia.

It could be, of course, that the wealthy person doesn't sleep because he lies awake in a state of anxiety about his investments. Perhaps the interest rate is going up ... or down ... depending on whether he is taking money out or putting money in at the moment. Perhaps the stock market is having a rough time, or the unit trusts have been disappointing, or an investment has failed. There's enough there to ensure he never gets enough shut-eye.

Actually, the Preacher is probably much more mundane in his thinking. He connects the insomnia of the rich with the richness of their food. The poor person sleeps sweetly 'whether he eats little or much', but the rich person cannot sleep because of his abundance. He can't sleep because he's eaten too much and those fabulous gourmet meals have been too rich for his delicate digestive system to stomach. He can't sleep because he's too fat and too full.

In 1923 Dr Martyn Lloyd-Jones was working as an assistant to Sir Thomas Horder, the eminent Harley Street physician and the King's doctor. One of his tasks was to re-classify his chief's case histories under their respective diseases. He discovered that as many as 70% of his private cases could not be classified under recognized medical criteria at all. Sir Thomas had written on so many of their notes observations such as 'Eats too much' or 'Drinks too much'. Medicine could help little when the flaw lay in the fundamental lifestyle.[1] It may have surprised the young Dr Lloyd-Jones, but such diagnoses would have come as no surprise to the Preacher in Ecclesiastes.

Is that too cynical a view of riches – the jaundiced view of a Preacher who doesn't have much himself and so delights in taking pot-shots at those he envies? Perhaps he says this because he has an axe to grind? Given the challenge, the Preacher continues his critique of wealth, perhaps a little bit more dispassionately.

What wealth pays (5:14-17)

When you carefully, coolly, and objectively look into wealth, what does it have to offer you? Sadly, as far as the Preacher is concerned, the balance sheet is firmly in the red. He does not ignore the assets and will investigate them thoroughly in the next chapter. But when you count up the income and expenditure account over all, he insists that you have not made any real profit. So what are these debits which are so great that they outweigh the profits?

There is no respect (5:13-14)

Some people treat money with great care. Perhaps they never had much as children and every penny counted. They learned to be frugal and to adopt the Protestant work ethic to an extreme degree. So in adult life they are very careful. They spend little on their own pleasure and are never guilty of impetuous buying or waste. They save prudently so that they will have enough for a rainy day. They invest wisely to obtain a judicious return on their capital. And then the company in which they have invested fails overnight, or the ravages of inflation eat away at their pension, and they are left with nothing.

Others handle money with reckless abandon. They seem to spend it as soon as they have it and they appear to take unwise risks with it. After all, taking risks is the only way to make 'real' money. Much of the time they seem to succeed. But there's no guarantee. Sir Freddie Laker took risks and for years seemed to have the Midas touch. In March 1981 his company made a profit of £3 million, but by February 1982 it was out of business.[2]

The point is that whether you are prudent and conservative in your approach to money or a reckless risk-taker it makes little difference. The end result is quite beyond your control. Wealth seems to be no respecter of persons. Either way you cannot be sure it is going to do you any good.

But the Preacher's concern is not only the destruction of wealth, it is also that the process of acquiring and losing wealth destroys the person. 'I have seen a grievous evil under the sun: wealth hoarded to the harm of its owner.'

Howard Hughes is an arch example of what the preacher has in mind. The wealthiest man in the world became an eccentric recluse at the end of his life. He was totally obsessed with his own health and suffered from paralysing phobias about germs. He lived in a darkened room, grew his hair long and had two-inch-long fingernails.

Or take Paul Getty as another example. His family were never free from feuding and his sons never felt he loved them or that he had time for them. He never found happiness or success in marriage and not one of those who worked for him had any respect for him in the end. A recent biography says his is the story of 'a wealth that afforded him no joy. Five marriages, five divorces. Two terrible deaths. And unforgiving, unrelenting miserliness .... A legend of luxury, lust and loneliness.'[3]

Mercifully, the effects of wealth are not normally so extreme. But in numerous subtle ways it can destroy the person who loves it. It shows little respect to its admirers, as a string of those who have suddenly won the football pools or the lottery can testify. So often tragedy has followed their windfall.

It is not the money that is evil in itself. Interestingly, the Preacher says that he had seen this evil 'under the sun'. He employs his code-words again. Money can be a gift from God. When treated as such, and therefore received with thanksgiving and used in stewardship, it need not have these harmful effects. But when used without reference to God it can be quite destructive.

There is no profit (5:15-17)
In the long run you gain nothing. When the balance sheet is made up, the profit line reads 'zero-nil return', which is exactly where you started.

When you think of it, it's obvious. You're born with nothing, not even a stitch of clothes. And when you die you take nothing with you. Naked you came and naked you go. You may have had a lot of money through your hands in the meantime, but what good does it do you then?

I remember reading the newspaper headline when Howard

Hughes died. It claimed 'the richest man in the world died yesterday'. And I recall thinking that at that moment Howard Hughes was worth less that I was, which on my salary at the time was quite an achievement! For all his millions, he stood, like everyone else, naked before his Maker. There the real accounting was about to take place.

There is no justice (5:16)
The Preacher cries out in protest, 'It isn't right' (GNB). There are so many evils associated with money in one way or another that you want to fight back and say it shouldn't be like this. You want to try to change it so that the poor don't suffer, or so that money doesn't have such a destructive effect in the lives of those who have it, or so that it can be more trustworthy, or so that it can have an effect beyond the grave. But it's totally unresponsive. We can't do anything about it. We are simply left to cry in anguish, 'This too is a grievous evil.'

What wealth buys (6:1-9)
Surely there must be some advantages of being rich. Yes, there are, and the Preacher now turns to consider them. Above all, riches help you to live in style. Look at the checklist of specific items the Preacher mentions that contribute to that style.

A big family (6:3)
If you are wealthy you can afford to have lots of children and surround yourself with company. Life can be like a continuous party with someone always coming and going and always with some cause for celebration. Money would remove the messy side of family life. Nannies could take care of the nappies. You needn't get your hands dirty if you are rich. You can just enjoy the pleasant side. It could lead you to a real-life Hollywood glamour, with all those luscious dinner

parties. But the moment you have said that, the realization has dawned that maybe that's not what you want after all.

Those who are nowhere near the first division in wealth will often say 'It's the family that matters.' In spite of the mammoth and sad breakdown in family life today, many people still look to their families for comfort, security and fulfilment and they long to see their ideals and happiness realized there. Money isn't essential to achieve those ends, but it certainly helps.

Long life (6:3)

There is an indisputable connection between wealth and health. The poorer you are the greater the risk to your health. If you are unemployed you are liable to suffer from sickness more than those who are employed.

A 1986 report to the British Association by Professor Peter Townsend spoke of the widening health gap between rich and poor in the UK.[4] Twice as many deaths occurred among working-class men in the same age group. Those below or slightly above the poverty line had increased from 7.4 million in 1960 to 16.3 million in 1983. In poorer parts of Bristol the number of stillbirths and infant deaths was twice as high as in the well-to-do suburbs.

At the other end of the scale, if you are wealthy you can pamper yourself. You can afford to indulge and then pay to go to a health farm for a week of torture in order to repair the damage! You can afford to travel to the sun! You can afford the subscription to the golf club or to have your own swimming pool. You can afford the private medical insurance which will give you instant access to the best medical practitioners in the land when ever anything goes wrong with you.

Eammon Andrews once made the mistake of having Vidal Sassoon and Bob Geldof together on his chat show. Sassoon had made $60 million dollars the year before and was celebrating his sixtieth birthday, and he looked great. 'You know,' he said, 'nobody should let themselves go when they get to my age. You want to get out and exercise. I do four billion push-ups every day, and look at me.' He carried on talking about doing a few lengths of his pool every day, and working out in his gym and 'continued in this narcissistic Californian way' until Geldof could take it no longer and exploded. Most people, Geldof pointed out, were rather too busy trying to stay alive to be so self-obsessed in finding out the secret of eternal youth.[5]

Again, how frequently people say, 'it's your health that matters; as long as you have got that you can cope with most things!' Well, money helps you keep your health.

An ambitious personality (6:7)

The enigmatic reference of verse 7 probably means something like this. The rich person has ambition and drive and since they are never satisfied he just keeps going at it.

Rich people are the ones who get things done. They are the get-up-and-goers. They're the bosses. They have flair and initiative and take risks. They have confidence to know where they're going and jet around the world with a passport to everywhere. They have 'A' type personalities.

They're like Victor Kyam, who liked the razor he shaved with and so bought the company who manufactured them. His autobiography, which was at the top of the bestseller list for several weeks, is called *Go For It*.[6] There is something we admire about such people. They've got backbone. They're successful. And wealth helps to breed more success.

A good education (6:8)

Wealth means you can wear the right old-school tie. The advantages of that are both direct, in that you probably have the right contacts through the old-boy network, and also indirect, in that it gives you a certain social competence and trains you in how to conduct yourself. You have, therefore, the edge when it comes to interviews, and you know how to speak to your elders and betters. Others, of course, can learn such social skills, but the Preacher is convinced that their poorer backgrounds will inevitably show and prove a stumbling-block to them. It's the right breeding that matters, and wealth helps to provide it.

How wealth fails (6:1-9)

Right through the recitation of the advantages the Preacher threads his doubts and his qualifications. Yes, of course, money matters. But you may have it all and still be desperately unhappy. Money does not bring fulfilment in itself, and cannot. At the risk of labouring the point, let us look at the negative thread about money which he weaves into these verses.

Money does not bring enjoyment (6:2-6)

It is God who gives a person enjoyment in life, not money. You may have the money and no joy, or the money and joy. You may have no money and joy or no money and misery. It's not the money that makes the difference but God.

Why is God so cruel as to withhold enjoyment? Simply so that we do not depend on false crutches and worship false idols. If we had great contentment through money we would dispense with God, thinking we had no need of him.

As the Preacher reflects on this he is gripped by a dark and deepening despair. It is better to be a stillborn child than to be caught up in this meaningless nonsense. Why be so preoccupied with the desire for things and allow yourself to be under their tyranny to make money for the major part of your life when, in the end, it makes no difference at all whether you were rich or poor? When you die you take the same route as everyone else, whatever their social background or income bracket may be.

Money doesn't help us deal with our ultimate enemy, death. Cecil Rhodes was, according to his biographer John Flint, 'wealthy beyond imagination, secure in the experience of enormous power, admired at home and abroad and lived in simple elegance amid natural beauty. Surely he was satisfied? Not so. Rhodes feared death.... He would have given all that he possessed, he once told Bramwell Booth, son of the founder of the Salvation Army, to be able to believe in an afterlife. 'Happy? I, Happy? Good God No!'[7]

Money does not bring fulfilment (6:9)
Money will hold out many promises. It will advertise itself as the way to contentment and fulfilment. But it will never deliver its promise. Fulfilment is always just out of reach, just around the corner. It's always going to come with the next million or thousand that you make. But it never does. The verdict of the Preacher is that 'his appetite is never satisfied'.

Money does not bring achievement (6:9)
Once more the verdict is pronounced. 'This too is meaningless, a chasing after the wind.' There are too many biographies and autobiographies of the rich and famous to justify that statement for us to have any need to support it further. You may have got everything, done everything, gone everywhere – but in the end it's nothing.

When wealth helps
Can the Preacher really be so negative about wealth as he seems? Is there nothing good to be said about it which he does not immediately ruin with an 'Ah, but ...'? Surely he has overstated his case. Not only has wealth a positive role to play but there are many people who have it who do not find

that it fails them in the way the Preacher seems to think is inevitable.

Enjoy God's gifts (5:18-20)
The point is simple. There is no automatic enjoyment to be found in wealth. It does not have the power to bestow enjoyment on those who possess it. Such power belongs to God alone.

The Preacher readily admits that he knows wealthy people who have no difficulty in enjoying their money. They even enjoy the burdens of responsibility and lifestyle which go with it. What is their secret? In a word, God. He gives them the gift of enjoyment (*verse 19*) and he keeps them 'occupied with gladness of heart' (*verse 20*).

At first sight such a comment seems at best a mystery and at worst an injustice. At best we want to ask why it is that some are given this ability to enjoy wealth while others are denied it. What formula does God use in deciding who falls into which camp? Can we crack the formula and thus perhaps defeat it? At worst we want to protest that God has no right arbitrarily to decide like this and therefore to withhold enjoyment from many.

But the Preacher is not intending to be so obscure. The answer lies much more within our own power. He simply means that if you allow God in, if you reverence him and live in the light of his commands, then enjoyment will come.

So many people find no enjoyment in money because they make it their god. So it usurps the place in their lives which belongs to God alone. No wonder it turns sour in their mouths. But if God reigns supreme in your life then money takes its proper place and you are free to enjoy it.

Think of all the implications. For a start your goals are different. You no longer serve the goal of making money, but of glorifying God. So you are not enslaved by it. Making a profit is a by-product of something far more worth while. Then believing in God affects your attitudes. No longer are you grasping, but rather, because you seek to imitate him, you become more open-handed and generous. The spin-offs of that in terms of relationships certainly help to make life more enjoyable. Then, serious belief in God means that anxiety goes out of your life because you trust that he is in control and knows what's best. So you don't lie awake at night wondering what the stock market is going to do tomorrow. And so we could go on.

So, God is not playing a cat-and-mouse game with you. He does not sadistically deny you the pleasure you seek just at the moment you think you've found it. He simply says that the only way to find real pleasure, whether you are wealthy or not, is to find it through giving your life over to God. No other way is possible. We're just not built that way.

Once you do put him in control, the gift of enjoyment comes.

Accept God's place (6:9)

The old saying claims that the grass is always greener on the other side. And we foolishly believe it! But the Preacher has a greater wisdom to teach. It is easy to have a roving eye which persistently tells you that someone else has got a much better deal than you have, or that living somewhere else would lead to contentment. But rather than solving your problems such an attitude may be the cause of them.

Deep down you know that unless *you* change, a change in your fortunes or circumstances will make no difference. The fault does not lie out there but inside. To change your environment and go after all that you desire, even to fulfil all your ambitions, would, at most, only attack the symptoms of your discontent.

The Preacher recommends, instead, that you do something

about yourself and learn contentment. 'Better what the eye sees than the roving of the appetite.' In other words, accept what God has given you and count it dear. It may not be much but it can be a source of greater happiness than striving after what has not come your way.

Put another way, you must be content with the place that God has given to you. If he wishes to change it he will. Paul gives the same instruction to young Christians at Corinth, whose newfound freedom in Christ gave them desires for social emancipation and increased status, which soon became nothing more than worldly ambition (1 Cor. 7:21-24). Contentment is not related to either your social or your economic position. It is related to your desires and they, in turn, are related to your trust in God.

Recognize God's sovereignty (6:10)

The Preacher now puts an edge on his words about accepting your place. 'No man can contend with one who is stronger then he.' We may not like the reminder that we are only creatures, subject to the power of our Maker, but those are the facts of the situation.

We, who feel so important and proud, so strong and prestigious, need to be reminded frequently how puny we are. We are really weak, vulnerable and dependent, and have no hope at all of ultimately succeeding in any fight we pick with the Almighty. His word is the one that counts. We cannot contend with him.

That being so, it is useless to protest against his will for us. If we argue, we shall lose. If we kick, we shall only hurt ourselves. It is far better to accept his chosen pathway and to try to discern his will and purposes as we travel it.

But the picture of God as 'one who is stronger than man' is not presented to ensure that we are reduced to weak resignation. It is not there to blackmail us into feeble compliance, or to knock the stuffing out of us. It is there to reveal the truth. God is stronger than we are and stronger than anything else we might look on as worthy of our worship, money included. So he, and he alone, deserves the adoration of our hearts and the obedience of our wills. Money is a worthless and unworthy idol.

It is amazing how much time we spend making money, investing it, or spending it. It occupies so much of our waking thoughts. It easily takes over. But it is foolish to let it do so. Money must be dethroned in order that God may be enthroned.

One Christmas, as we were visiting my aged grandmother, a lady whom we had never met called on her at the same time. She was in her early sixties. As the conversation progressed something of her story came out. She had just been through the most tragic year of her whole life. She and her husband had been on holiday earlier that year in Spain, where he had dropped dead. It was totally unexpected. She flew back to Britain with his body for his burial, only to walk into further tragedy.

Not long before, she and her husband had put their life savings into one new investment fund on the recommendation of a man who was thought to be utterly reliable. It turned out that he was fraudulent, and she was greeted with the news that she had lost everything. The man concerned was wanted by the police for a string of similar offences and had fled overseas. There was no hope that anything could be recovered.

She suddenly found herself without husband and without money. The peaceful years of retirement of which they had long dreamed had overnight become a nightmare. She had to sell her house in order to exist, and had moved to a much smaller place where she had to try to pick up the pieces. It is bad enough for any widow to move while still grieving and to have to face rebuilding a home without a man around the house to do all those little, simple practical jobs he had always done. But it was far worse for a woman in her position.

But I tell you I have never met a happier woman. Her serenity was not superficial. She felt the pain of loss keenly. She was not naively triumphalistic. She hurt. But she recognized the sovereignty of God in her life. He was in control and she trusted him. She didn't worry about the things that others had made into idols. God was all that mattered. She knew that in sickness or in health, in poverty or in wealth, God could give the gift of enjoyment. He had given it to her and she was enjoying it.

Enjoyment of life doesn't depend on your circumstances, or your bank balance, or your ambitiousness, or your status, or your success. It depends on God. If God wants to make you rich, he will. And he can give you the power to enjoy your wealth. If God wants to keep you poor, he's able to do that too. And he's able to let you enjoy it just as much.

So don't build your life on money, but rather on the living God.

References
1. Iain H. Murray, *D. Martyn Lloyd-Jones: The First Forty Years, 1899-1939* (Banner of Truth, 1982), p.62.
2. Jeffrey Robinson, *The Risk Takers* (George Allen and Urwin, 1985), p. 9.
3. Russell Miller, *The House of Getty* (Coroner Books, 1985).
4. Peter Townsend, quoted in *The Times*, 4 September 1986.
5. Bob Geldof, *Is That It?* (Sidgewick & Jackson, 1986), p. 184.
6. Victor Kyam, *Go For It* (Collins, 1986).
7. John Flint, *Cecil Rhodes* (Hutchinson, 1976), p. 175.

7

HOW TO CHANGE YOUR APPEARANCE
7:1-8:1

A good name is better than fine perfume, and the day of death better than the day of birth.

[2]It is better to go to a house of mourning
    than to go to a house of feasting,
for death is the destiny of every man;
    the living should take this to heart.
[3]Sorrow is better than laughter,
    because a sad face is good for the heart.
[4]The heart of the wise is in the house of mourning
    but the heart of fools is in the house of pleasure.
[5]It is better to heed a wise man's rebuke
    than to listen to the song of fools.
[6]Like the crackling of thorns under the pot,
    so is the laughter of fools.
This too is meaningless.

[7]Extortion turns a wise man into a fool,
    and a bribe corrupts the heart.
[8]The end of a matter is better than its beginning,
    and patience is better than pride.
[9]Do not be quickly provoked in your spirit,
    for anger resides in the lap of fools.
[10]Do not say, "Why were the old days better than these?"
    For it is not wise to ask such questions.

[11]Wisdom, like inheritance, is a good thing
    and benefits those who see the sun.
[12]Wisdom is a shelter
    as money is a shelter,
    but the advantage of knowledge is this:
that wisdom preserves the life of its possessor.

[13]Consider what God has done:

Who can straighten
    what he has made crooked?
[14]When times are good be happy;
    but when times are bad, consider:
God has made the one
    as well as the other.
Therefore, a man cannot discover
    anything about his future.

[15]In this meaningless life of mine I have seen both of these:
    a righteous man perishing in his righteousness,
        and a wicked man living long in his wickedness.
[16]Do not be over-righteous,
    neither be overwise –
    why destroy yourself?
[17]Do not be overwicked,
    and do not be a fool –
    why die before your time?
[18]It is good to grasp the one
    and not let go of the other.
    The man who fears God will avoid all extremes.
[19]Wisdom makes one wise man more powerful
    than ten rulers in a city.
[20]There is not a righteous man on earth
    who does what is right and never sins.
[21]Do not pay attention to every word people say,
    or you may hear your servant cursing you –
[22]for you know in your heart
    that many times you yourself have cursed others.
[23]All this I tested by wisdom and I said,
"I am determined to be wise" –
    but this was beyond me.
[24]Whatever wisdom may be,
    it is far off and most profound –
    who can discover it?
[25]So I turned my mind to understand,
    to investigate and to search out wisdom

and the scheme of things
and to understand the stupidity of wickedness
    and the madness of folly.

[26]I find more bitter than death
    the woman who is a snare,
whose heart is a trap
    and whose hands are chains.
The man who pleases God will escape her,
    but the sinner she will ensnare.

[27]"Look," says the Teacher, "this is what I have discovered:

"Adding one thing to another to discover the scheme of things –
[28]while I was still searching but not finding –
I found one upright man among a thousand,
    but not one upright woman among them all.
[29]This only have I found:
    God made mankind upright,
    but men have gone in search of many schemes."
[8:1]Who is like the wise man?
    Who knows the explanation of things?
Wisdom brightens a man's face
    and changes its hard appearance.

Some people will go to extraordinary lengths to change their appearance. Sharon Wood was born with some facial deformity as a result of her mother having taken Debendox, an anti-morning-sickness pill, during her pregnancy. Sadly, two bony lumps protruded from her forehead and she had an unusually wide space between her eyes. The result was that Sharon was taunted by other children and ostracized as ugly.

To spare her that stigma, Sharon, at the age of eight, was subjected to a nine-hour operation. It involved cutting out 18mm of bone from the centre of her face with a pneumatic drill, hammer and chisel, pushing her brain an inch or two out of the way, swinging round the facial bones, and remodelling her nose using a piece of bone removed from her hip.[1]

For most of us the quest to improve our appearance is not so dramatic. But we regard our appearance as important. So every year we spend millions on cosmetics to take away the wrinkles and hide the ageing process, to make us look healthier and to lift the drooping parts of our faces. In 1996 we spent £6,584,000 on toiletries alone – much more than we spent on many other things which may be deemed more essential.[2]

And yet there is a problem. However much we spend on such cosmetics the change they make is only ever skin-deep. The change is only ever superficial, even artificial, for we ourselves haven't changed at all. We even use the word 'cosmetic' in precisely that way; to talk about a change which is all show and not real.

There is another approach we could take and it's one which many have found to work. That is to bring about changes on the inside and let them work towards the outside. Changes on the inside can have a dramatic effect on our looks. We all know how the alcoholic or the drug addict or the person suffering from stress looks years older than he or she is. But perhaps we do not sufficiently appreciate that being right on the inside can also have a visible effect on the outside. Of course it's not a guaranteed way of finding the secret of eternal youth. Nonetheless, what we're like on the inside is not unconnected with what we're like on the outside.

Ecclesiastes 7:1-8:1 is all about how we look. The Preacher begins this part of his argument by saying that 'a sad face is good for the heart' (7:3). Then he comes to the climax of his argument and says that 'wisdom brightens a man's face and changes its hard appearance' (8:1). So how do you change your appearance and get a bright face?

These are immensely complex verses and we cannot do anything more than give a bird's-eye view of their teaching. But for all their complexity they have a connecting thread in the subject of wisdom. It is by living wisely that your appearance can be improved. But what is wise living? How can we live wisely? Once we begin to unpack the Preacher's answer to those questions we soon discover that his teaching is deep, that what he proposes is demanding and that the changes which will result are anything but cosmetic. He speaks of four broad areas.

The tough side of life: value it (7:1-6)

We usually think that the way to be happy and to have a lovely, rosy, smiling face is to have a trouble-free existence. If only we could avoid suffering, misfortune, bereavement, being rebuked or put down, all would be well. Life would be swinging, we would be carefree and the happiness would show all over our faces. Some people float blissfully through life, managing to avoid all the obstacles that are strewn on most people's paths. But they are very much the exception, and often they are so superficial that they don't notice what's going on much. So they not only miss the knocks but miss many of the pleasures of life too.

The picture of a blissful, carefree life is not only unreal, it's not the way to achieve happiness. The Preacher suggests that it is far better to be realistic about life and reflect on its hard experiences that it is to try to escape them. And to drive home his point he lets rip a volley of sharp comparisons that on first hearing cause us to recoil. The first of these, in verse 1, that a good reputation is better than deodorants, is mild and humorous. But then he says:

> Death is better than life
> Fasting is better than feasting
> Sorrow is better than laughter
> Mourning is better than pleasure
> Rebuke is better than flattery.

Tremendous! He sounds like a real killjoy.

But hear him out. We know he's not a killjoy from what he has written elsewhere. So what is he trying to say? He's saying that we will get on much better in life if we are realistic about it and accept that it is going to have its tough side. What is more, he's saying that if you stop and think, you will find that it's on that tough side of life that we learn wisdom. Some of those nasty things are actually better for us than the smooth, pleasurable experiences of life.

If we are honest we would have to admit he is right. We may not value the sorrows, pain, bereavements and disappointments of life but it's when we are in those situations that we learn most and grow most. It's the hammer, pounding on the piece of metal on the anvil, that shapes it into a beautiful piece of art. It's the fire that makes the tool strong and reliable, ensuring that it won't break when you need it most. It's the metal, tested and tried, that will not fail you when under pressure and tension. And it is by being in the tough situations that we become stronger and equipped to cope with reality.

Charles Spurgeon confessed, 'I am afraid that all the grace I have gotten out of my comfortable and easy times and happy hours might almost lie on a penny. But the good that I received from my sorrows and pains and griefs is altogether incalculable. What do I not owe to the hammer and the anvil, the fire and the file. Affliction is the best bit of furniture in my house.'

The Preacher pleads with us to have the same attitude and to approach these tough experiences wisely. It is not wise to deny them and pretend they have not happened. It is not wise to try to run away from them. It is not wise to protest angrily against them. It is not wise to laugh them off. Wisdom calls us to accept them and reflect on them, and to see what they have to teach us.

A wise approach to life's experiences will do two things. First, *it will teach us to face the reality of death* (verse 2).

'Death is the destiny of every man' and there is little point in pretending otherwise. What sex was to the Victorians, death is to us. It's the great unmentionable subject. We distance ourselves from it by taking our dying relatives out of our homes and by putting them in hospitals or hospices. Many people no longer know how to express the emotions of grief at a funeral service. But it's useless to run away from death, for, sooner or later, we shall all experience it. Death is a true reality with which we need to come to terms.

Secondly, *it will help us to discover a true perspective on life* (verse 6). Harold Kushner has commented, 'I believe that it is not dying that people are afraid of. Something else, something more unsettling and more tragic than dying frightens us. We are afraid of never having lived, of coming to the end of our days with the sense that we were never really alive, that we never figured out what life was for.[3] The tough experiences of life may help us to live by helping us to evaluate things differently and to gain a wiser perspective than we might otherwise have had. It teaches us to cling onto some things more dearly and let go of other things more freely.

It's an old preacher's story, but it makes the point and it's supposed to be true. One woman on the sinking *Titanic* shunned the offer of a lifeboat while she rushed back to her cabin. Once she got there she did not reach for her jewels or her money. She reached for some oranges. They were of far more value to her when she was cast adrift in the ocean and facing the peril on the high seas than the trinkets of high society.

So, warns the Preacher, it is with life. Laughter (verse 6) may seem to be fun. It's at parties you find most enjoyment. They make a lot of noise, like burning twigs, and draw a lot of attention to themselves. But parties come and parties go. They are fine while they last but once they are over, the one who was the life and soul of the party often goes home empty and alone. We need to discover what will endure and be of lasting significance. Suffering often teaches us what is most valuable in life and what will last to eternity.

Adelaide Ann Procter knew that when she wrote:

> I thank thee, Lord, that all our joy
>   Is touched with pain;
> That shadows fall on brightest hours,
>   That thorns remain:
> So that earth's bliss may be our guide,
>   And not our chain.
> For thou who knowest, Lord, how soon
>   Our weak heart clings,
> Hast given us joys, tender and true,
>   Yet all with wings;
> So that we see gleaming on high,
>   Diviner things.[4]

The value of pain and pressure as a means of producing life has been dramatically illustrated by Philip Yancey. He draws us into the experience as he writes:

> Your world is dark, safe and secure. You are bathed in warm liquid cushioned from shock. You do nothing for yourself; you are fed automatically, and a murmuring heartbeat assures you that someone larger than you fills all your needs. Your life consists of simple waiting – you're not sure what to wait for, but any change seems far away and scary. You meet no sharp objects, no pain, no threatening adventures. A fine existence.
>
> One day you feel a tug. The walls are falling in on you. Those soft cushions are now pulsing and beating against you, crushing you downwards. Your body is bent double, your limbs twisted and wrenched. You're falling upside down. For the first time in your life you feel pain. You're in a sea of rolling matter. Then more pressure, almost too intense to bear. Your head is squeezed flat, and you are pushed harder, harder into a dark tunnel. Oh, the pain. Noise. More pressure. You hurt all over. You hear a groaning sound and an awful, sudden fear rushes in on you. It is happening – your world is collapsing. You're sure it's the end. You see a piercing,

blinding light. Cold rough hands pull at you. A painful slap. Waaaahhhh! Congratulations! You've just been born.[5]

Value the tough side of life. It's a great life-giver.

The trip-wires of life: avoid them (7:7-10)

The Preacher certainly does not pretend that learning wisdom is going to be easy. In particular he notes that there are four temptations which will conspire, either singly or together, to trip us up and cause us to live anything but wise lives.

The point of noting them is so that we can be more readily alert for them. They need not take us by surprise and land us flat on our faces. Furthermore, if we identify them now as potential trip-wires we shall not be able to make lame excuses once they have caught us in their trap. We shall have to be more honest and admit that the fault is ours in no small measure.

Here they are.

Extortion (7:7)

'Everyone has his price', we say. And sadly this low estimate of mankind proves true too often to dismiss it as sheer pessimism. People are corrupted very easily. Backhanders, bribes, favours, call them what you will, are common precisely because they work. The recent history of government and of business is riddled with incidents which show how easy it is for crafty people to buy their way into positions of influence or buy their firms into lucrative contracts while feathering their own nest at the same time. The issue of sleaze was a major issue for John Major's Parliament.

But such a path is anything but wise. It may look attractive on the surface, and you may even be able to argue that you are doing good to others, by securing them their jobs, if you bend the rules a little. But in the end it is a road which is nothing other than foolish. When it all comes out you find you have lost everything – money, business, freedom and respect. The wise way, even if it is the harder way, is one of absolute undeviating integrity.

Impatience (7:8)
Here's a lesson for the age of instant everything! 'The end of the matter is better than the beginning, and patience is better than pride.' We are so used to getting quick results that we are losing the ability to endure. Unless we can see the end product overnight we don't stick with it. We throw in the towel. Most of us can think of times when we have set out to establish some project but have quickly got discouraged and given up. The grand plans we had, and which no doubt we talked about to others, then condemn us and make us look foolish.

In our more sensible moments, we know that virtually anything worth while takes time to develop. No concert pianist learns to play Beethoven's concertos overnight. No pop musician reaches stardom without months, if not years, of hard work. No comedian reaches the big time without working the clubs first. No research scientist makes the big break-through without years of scientific training, and painstaking, even fruitless, research beforehand.

We can all start something, but can we stick at it? If we are among the wise then we must learn to endure, to persevere, and, to use an old-fashioned word, to be steadfast. The world is littered with fools who quickly gave up what they began and who then turned just as easily to something else, only perhaps, before long, to jettison that too. Fads and fashions come and go very quickly in modern society. And all too easily we swallow the spirit of the age and reproduce it in other spheres where we cannot afford to be so superficial.

Jesus warned his disciples that before they threw in their lot with him they should count the cost carefully. He told a parable about the need to do some detailed calculations before you build a tower or before you wage war against an enemy (Luke 14:28-33). Would that Christian people took him seriously! The Christian church at the present time is strewn with 'fools'. We suffer badly from people who initiate Christian work with high hopes and great promises but quickly get tired and chuck it in. No-one pretends it's easy. But what these people lack is stamina. The church needs more people with the discipline of the long distance runner and fewer with the character of the sprinter. This saying of the preacher is one which the church, let alone anyone else, desperately needs to take to heart.

Anger (7:9)
One can see why the preacher should mention anger next. There are lots of perplexities and discouragements if you are doing any serious work and it's not surprising that anyone in that situation should want to hit out against them and want to fight back. Things will go wrong and, even more to the point, people will let you down. It's in us all to let rip when that happens.

But, again, he asks if such a response is wise. Far from being a constructive solution to an already difficult problem, it may cause it to deteriorate still further. Rather than motivating people to come and cooperate with us, it may drive them away further. Rather than helping us to see the situation more objectively, it will distort our vision more. Anger is deceitful. It gives us the satisfaction of a quick emotional release but it does nothing to change the situation for the better. In fact the quick temper really demonstrates what others already suspected, that we are really a bit foolish.

The wise person will learn to discipline his temper and emotions. It may not be easy for him to do so but he will struggle with it until he has mastered himself.

Nostalgia (7:10)

How glad I am that the Bible gives such an unequivocal verdict on those painful people who are always living in the past! 'Do not say, "Why were the old days better than these?" For it is not wise to ask such questions.'

Yet it is a question which is being constantly asked, especially in the church. 'Why are there no great preachers around like there used to be?' 'We remember when the church was packed with seats down the aisles; why can't you fill it now?' 'We can't stand this modern music. Give us back the old anthems and the lovely organ voluntaries.' And so on, we've all heard it and many of us have said it.

But such questions show that we are secret escapists. We would prefer to escape the harsh realities of the present world and take a holiday in history rather than grapple with the world as it is now and deal with it as it is today.

We need to remember that all of us look back with rose-tinted spectacles. We have selective memories which highlight the good from the past and which unobtrusively filter out the bad. We think it was better then. But maybe we didn't think it was so good at the time. When we were living through those times we now think so good, we were full of moans and groans. It's only time that has hallowed them. There is room for a bit more honesty about our yesteryears.

Such honesty will enable us to live in the present. If we keep saying, 'Oh, if only it was like it was', we are going down a path that the Bible declares to be foolish. Wisdom demands that we be realistic about the world in which we live today and that we come to terms with it.

The preacher is certainly hitting the nail on the head as far as the church is concerned. So much about the church gives the impression that it is a museum. Its buildings look like museums, its members behave as if they were antiquarians, and they speak in those hushed artificial and reverent tones you associate with museums. Sadly it means that the God they exhibit often seems to others nothing more than a relic from the past. But our God is ever contemporary. And he desires a discipleship which is for today.

Tripping over those wires should ring alarm bells for us but they often fail to do so. The alarm should ring because they are all forms of escapism. Extortion is an escape from responsibility. Impatience gives in too easily and is short on reality. Anger says the fault lies in everyone else. Nostalgia says, 'Let's escape to the past which was more safe and secure.' But such escapism is the very opposite of wise living.

The think-tank of life: prize it (7:11-19)

Having warned of the dangers of folly, the Preacher now sets out the advantages of wisdom. Wisdom has nothing to do with academic prowess. People who fail their GCEs may be very wise, whereas we know for a fact that many Ph.Ds totally lack wisdom. Wisdom is living reverently before God. It is to fear God above anything else. It is to understand your world and your own life from God's viewpoint. It is to reflect prudently on one's experience from the perspective of divine revelation.

In effect it means living the way God has shown us in the Bible. That is not to recommend an unintelligent application of the Bible to our modern world. We need to approach the Bible itself with discernment, not apply all of its teaching literally to our very different context today. For instance, I don't believe that living wisely would mean that we stone adulterers or count those in contact with dead bodies as unclean. We need to ask how the original readers would have understood what was written, to dig deep to the principles which are involved, and then to translate their application to today's society. But, whatever the qualification, we must insist that it is living by the Bible that will lead to wisdom.

Why is wisdom so important? The Preacher sets out its advantages.

Wisdom provides protection (7:1-12)
If we are sensible we save for a rainy day. There may come a time when things go wrong, and if we've got some money in the bank, or if we've just received an inheritance, we are able to cope. It acts as a good buffer against difficulty. It's the same with wisdom. It is 'a good thing', it benefits, it 'is a shelter' and 'preserves the life of its possessor'.

If you possess wisdom then you won't be thrown headlong when you stumble over life's pitfalls. Panic, despair, stupidity won't seize you and instantly make the matter worse. But you will be able to understand the situation more coolly and so handle it better.

Imagine that there is a sudden and tragic death in the family. I would not wish to trivialize the pain of bereavement or to stunt the right and proper process of grief. Yet the wise person realizes that sooner or later we will all die, and although the circumstances of this particular passing may be very unfortunate, death in some shape or form would have come eventually. The wise person also believes in the resurrection and has hope that death is not the end. The foolish person harbours resentment and bitterness and won't let the person go, or refuses to come to terms with his or her death. Wisdom saves us from ourselves.

Or take temptation as another example. The wise person knows what is right and what is wrong, and, when faced with the temptation, knows that he does not have to give into it. The Bible is full of verses assuring us that we can resist temptation successfully (such as Psalm 119:9, 11 and 1 Corinthians 10:13), and many have proved them to be true. So the wise person turns to God to gain strength from him.

The fool goes along with temptation and then suffers the consequences afterwards. When we do sin, wisdom leads us to face the fact squarely, confess it and put the matter right with God (1 John 1:9), thus saving us from worse problems, like the ones David admitted in Psalms 32 and 51 where he looked back on his earlier refusal to face up to his sin.

So wisdom helps to hedge us against the stormy blasts of life.

Wisdom provides perspective (7:13-18)
It gives us perspective both in relation to our ordinary lives and also in relation to our spiritual lives.

Perspective about ordinary life (7:13-14). Everyone of us comes across puzzles and riddles in life that we cannot sort out. There are many circumstances which we cannot understand. 'Who can straighten what he has made crooked?' We wish we could, but frankly have to admit that much of it is beyond us.

Wisdom will prevent us from getting bogged down by these puzzles. Some people are so wrapped up in the enigmas of life that they never live. Some are so intimidated by the problems that they are petrified. But the Preacher invites us to look at things another way. 'Consider', he says, 'what God has done.' Your life is not the outworking of blind fate and you are not the product of random chance. Behind your life is a sovereign God who is over all things and in control of all things. He may not have directly caused every difficulty and problem but he is quite capable of turning them all into good. He has a great track record for doing just that. Ask Joseph (Gen. 50:20), or listen to Paul in Romans 8:28. That puts things in a different light.

So when times are good, be happy. When times are bad, still trust. God has made the sunny days, but he remains faithful through the rainy days. The washdays of life belong to him as much as the holidays. The times of success come from God, and he uses the times of failure too. Health and promotion are his gift, but equally sickness and unemployment may be his tool.

Wisdom leads you to see it all as under his control. How different that is from many people who never think of God until something goes wrong and then instantly blame him for it. Wisdom suggests that we trace his hand in all of life, not just the good bits. As Richard Baxter put it:

> Take what he gives
> And praise him still
> Through good or ill
> Who ever lives.[6]

Perspective about spiritual life (7:15-18). The next concern which the Preacher voices comes as something of a shock. When you first hear it, it almost seems a straight-forward piece of secular advice. But any astute observer of the contemporary church scene will quickly come to appreciate the wisdom of his words. Ignorance of them has often meant that people have built a time-fuse into their spiritual lives which has exploded some time later with disastrous results. How many pastoral heartaches could have been avoided if only these words had been heeded.

The first matter where perspective is needed in spiritual life is mentioned in verse 15. In spite of all the value of living wisely, the Preacher admits that there is no iron spiritual law in operation in this world. It simply is not true that the wise will automatically prosper and the wicked will automatically suffer. That's why the 'prosperity movement', with its teaching that following Christ will bring you wealth, is so wrong. No slick formula for success exists and anyone who pretends it does is deluded. The gospel of prosperity is a cruel deception.

The Bible itself gives us plenty of illustrations of the way the righteous suffer. Think of Job or Jesus. It also knows the reverse, and expresses the agony of the righteous who see the wicked prosper, as in Psalm 73. Present-day experience is just the same. Archbishop Janini Luwum suffered a violent and unjust death at the hands of Idi Amin while the tyrant still lives. We must be prepared to accept either lot in life. Wisdom will help us to take either in our stride.

The second matter where perspective is needed is over the intensity of our religious convictions. Verse 16 addresses this issue in a startling way. 'Do not be over-righteous ... why destroy yourself?'

The Gospels are full of people who were 'over-righteous' and they were all found ranged against Christ and leading the opposition against him. Pharisees, full of self-righteousness, are an unlovely sight. They know the rules and keep them. But they live imprisoned and inhibited lives. They impose the rules on others and look down on the masses from their position of spiritual superiority. All they really do is keep the letter of the law while constantly breaching its spirit. They succeed in putting people's backs up, but they do not succeed in winning anyone for their religion by love. Such an approach is self-destructive.

With the exciting renewal of the church which we are currently experiencing, there is a danger in some quarters of being 'over-righteous'. Some are so spiritually intense as to be unreal. Some are so concerned to be keeping every scruple of the law, or so introspective in hunting down sin within, or so concerned to distance themselves from the world, that they have set themselves on a dangerous course. Sooner or later they will blow their spiritual gasket. And that will bring their spiritual lives to a messy end.

So some Christians even refuse to go on holiday, believing it to be a waste of time and money and an indulgence of the flesh. Some refuse to turn to a doctor when ill, on the grounds that that would indicate lack of faith. Some refuse to permit Christmas trees, seeing them as symbols of a pagan festival. Others will not allow a child's imagination to be stimulated by fiction (because it is not 'true'), or by conjuring (because that smacks of magic). There is little enjoyment of God's creation in such an approach. Sooner or later the pressure cooker will blow up and splatter the contents around the kitchen.

The third point on which perspective is needed is the other side of the coin (verse 17). The Preacher's cautions about being too spiritual cannot be taken to mean that we don't have to worry about sin and are free to live how we like. Not at all. Wickedness is also destructive, as the drug addict, the murderer and a host of others who have given in to it show. So, the Preacher equally warns us against letting our native sin run its course.

He is not pleading for moderation in spiritual matters so much as asking that we see the dangers of excesses on both sides. Holiness matters, so don't be a fool. But equally humanity matters, so don't be a spiritual prig. The wise person sees the dangers on both sides (verse 18), and walks between them.

Wisdom provides power (7:19)

The last advantage of wisdom, which is mentioned in this passage, is that it gives a person strength. A single wise person, it is claimed, will have more power than the collective wisdom of the city fathers. Setting aside our feelings that in the case of some local-government leaders that's not claiming much, what does the Preacher mean?

He means that we will have a personal strength within us if we live wisely. We shall have inner resources to cope with life's tragedies and not cave in when the winds blow. We shall have an inner discipline which will be worth far more than outward restraints. They merely produce conformity, and never really change our behaviour or motives. When the constraints are removed we quickly revert to sinful behaviour. If we live wisely we will have an integrity which will stand us in good stead when others are trimming their sails to the wind. That is real power.

The taunting side of life: accept it (7:20–8:1)

If the advantages of wisdom are so great and so obvious, why don't we all pursue it with all our strength? Ecclesiastes never leaves reality very far behind, and now, having extolled the virtues of wisdom, the Preacher returns to the world in which we live and in which wisdom is hard to find. Don't imagine, he says, that if you want to live wisely you are going to get a lot of help. You're not. You won't be popular. You won't even be in the majority. There will be few around to encourage you. But don't let that throw you off course. Be prepared for the taunts that you will receive.

Somewhat depressingly he comments on what he has seen. His commentary has two major themes.

Righteousness is elusive (7:20-22, 26-29)

He claims that he has not seen anyone who is righteous on earth. It may be that he is talking in general terms, rather than with statistical precision, as he makes this universal assertion. But I wouldn't be so sure. Verses 21 and 22 perhaps reveal that his condemnation is meant to be all-inclusive. He speaks of the unfortunate way in which, if we listen at keyholes, we may hear something unfortunate about ourselves. But then he confesses that before we condemn others for saying nasty things about us which are unwarranted, or for telling lies, we ought to remember that we have often said the same things about others. We have to admit that not even we are righteous; and if *we're* not, what hope is there for others!?

Perhaps we ought to comment on his apparently sexist remark in verse 26. While saying that he has found one righteous man in a thousand, he claims not to have found any righteous women at all. We may regret such a discriminatory remark today, but two things might help to explain why he said it. In comparison with other things written in his day about women, this remark is mild. In his cultural context it would not have been seen as offensive. Secondly, as R. Gordis has commented, when you work it out he does not claim much more for men. They are 'only one-tenth of one per cent better than women'![7]

More significantly, the Preacher is concerned about why righteousness is so scarce (verse 29). The fault does not lie with God, who made man upright in the first place. Rather, the responsibility lies with man. It is his restlessness, his scheming, his search for novelty, his waywardness, that have caused the problem. Far from being content with what God offered, man has gone his own way. So let's not blame God for the problems of the world. Let's look to ourselves and accept that responsibility lies at our doorstep.

Wisdom is elusive (7:23-25)
We could live righteously if we could live wisely but wisdom seems to be playing a perpetual game of hide-and-seek with us too. It is no more accessible than righteousness. So what's the use of trying?

The New Testament declares that wisdom is no longer as elusive as it was. With the coming of Jesus, God has brought it close to us. Paul says to the early Christians, 'You are in Jesus Christ, who has become for us wisdom from God' (1 Cor. 1:30).

God realized our predicament and has given us a solution. We do not have it within us to be wise ourselves. There is an inbuilt bias towards foolishness. But what we cannot be ourselves, we can be through faith in Jesus. We need to accept his forgiveness for our foolishness, and that frees us from the follies of the past. We can make him Lord, which gives us a new pattern of wisdom to follow. We can ask him to take over our lives and that means he will give us his Spirit's ability to live wisely. What we are not capable of ourselves we can receive from Christ, who longs to make us wise.

Our world has never known so much or been so intelligent. But where has it got us? Sad faces, hardened people, damaged lives and broken homes, disintegrating societies and nations at war, are the order of the day. All because we have the knowledge but not the wisdom we need.

Wisdom would make a real difference to us, not just a cosmetic change. All we need do is humbly to accept God's offer of wisdom in Jesus. But there's the stumbling-block. It is hard to admit that we have not got it within ourselves. We find it difficult to ask for help from outside. But if we do not, wisdom will remain elusive.

When we find wisdom, it will 'brighten our face' (8:1) and change our appearance, because a change will have taken place within. We shall then be in a better position to value the tough side of life, avoid the trip-wires of life, prize the think-tank of life and be undaunted by the taunting side of life.

References
1. *The Independent*, 23 March, 1987, p. 12.
2. Government Statistical Service: Consumer Expenditure.
3. Harold Kushner, *When All You Ever Wanted Isn't Enough* (Pan, 1987), p. 156.
4. The hymn, 'My God I thank thee, who hast made the earth so bright.'
5. Philip Yancey, *Where is God When It Hurts?* (Zondervan, 1978), pp. 179-183.
6. The hymn, 'Ye holy angels bright.'
7. Quoted in Michael Eaton, *Ecclesiastes* (*Tyndale Old Testament Commentaries*, IVP, 1983), p. 116.

8

A TALE TOLD BY AN IDIOT
8:2-17

Obey the king's command, I say, because you took an oath before God. Do not be in a hurry to leave the king's presence. [3]Do not stand up for a bad cause, for he will do whatever he pleases. [4]Since a king's word is supreme, who can say to him 'What are you doing?'

[5]Whoever obeys his command will come to no harm,
  and the wise heart will know the proper time and procedure.
[6]For there is a proper time and procedure for every matter,
  though a man's misery weighs heavily upon him.

[7]Since no man knows the future,
  who can tell him what is to come?
[8]No man has power over the wind to contain it;
  so no-one has power over the day of this death.
As no-one is discharged in time of war,
  so wickedness will not release those who practise it.

[9] All this I saw, as I applied my mind to everything done under the sun. There is a time when a man lords it over others to his own hurt. [10]Then too, I saw the wicked buried – those who used to come and go from the holy place and receive praise in the city where they did this. This too is meaningless.

[11]When the sentence for a crime is not quickly carried out the hearts of the people are filled with schemes to do wrong. [12]Although a wicked man commits a hundred crimes and still lives a long time, I know that it will go better with God-fearing men, who are reverent before God. [13]Yet because the wicked do not fear God, it will not go well with them, and their days will not lengthen like a shadow.

[14]There is something else meaningless that occurs on earth: righteous men who get what the wicked deserve, and wicked men who get what the righteous deserve. This too, I say, is meaningless. [15]So I commend the enjoyment of life, because nothing is better for a man under the sun than to eat, and drink and be glad. Then joy will accompany him in his

129

work all the days of the life God has given him under the sun.

[16]When I applied my mind to know wisdom and to observe man's labour on earth – his eyes not seeing sleep day or night – [17]then I saw all that God has done. No-one can comprehend what goes on under the sun. Despite all his efforts to search it out, man cannot discover its meaning. Even if a wise man claims he knows, he cannot really comprehend it.

Winston Churchill once said, 'Trying to maintain good relations with the Communists is like wooing a crocodile. You do not know whether to tickle it under the chin or beat it over the head. When it opens its mouth you cannot tell whether it's trying to smile or preparing to eat you up.' He also said once, when negotiating with them, 'It is a riddle wrapped in a mystery inside an enigma.'[1]

He might have been speaking more generally, for life is very much like that. It is like a Russian doll. You open up the first doll and inside is an identical one. You take that apart and there is another smaller copy of the same thing. So you prise open life's riddles, only to be faced by its mysteries. You just succeed in cracking them, or so you think, only to be confronted immediately by its enigmas. There seems to be no escape.

Ecclesiastes 8 is all about taking the Russian doll to pieces and confronting the enigmas you find. The chapter actually adopts two stances. The dominant one is that of living 'under the sun' (verses 9, 15, 17). It dwells on the frustrations you see from below. Woven into it, however, is a second stance which recognizes life 'above the sun' and which brings some answers from above.

Frustrations from below
Starting with the dominant stance, Mr Preacher tells us of four great enigmas in life which lead to total frustration.

The enigma of authority (8:2-8)

We would need to change the language. The Preacher talks of the king. We would speak not of the king but of the government. We may also do so initially with a sense of pride, for modern democratic government seems poles apart from ancient oriental despotism. And yet it soon becomes clear that our experience is not so different after all. We are often pulled in different directions. On the one hand we feel thankful that government is there and we recognise the many benefits which result from it. On the other hand we find it often gets in the way and is a menace. The Preacher admits to the same tensions. Look at the ambiguities he describes.

First, *he encourages our desire to obey the king (verse 2)*. The reason he gives is that 'you took an oath before God'. In a direct sense we probably no longer do so, unless we are part of the legislature or the magistracy and have sworn an oath of allegiance to the Queen. But the phrase points to a more general principle which does apply to us all. The oath before God points to the connection there is between government and God.

God knew that, just as there would need to be physical laws to provide the universe with coherence, so there would need to be social laws, institutions and organization to provide coherence in society, to enable fallen human beings to relate to one another with reasonable restraint, and to permit good to prevail. To that end he instituted governments. Romans 13:1-7 spells it out for us. And since it is God who has brought them into being, our attitude to them says something about our attitude to him.

We may wonder sometimes how God could have ordained particular governments. But the Bible is more concerned about the principle of the matter than its practice. For all our frustrations with government, try to imagine what the absence of government would be like. If we lived in a society where everyone did what was right in his own eyes, anarchy and chaos would reign. We only have to look at the chaos caused in several places recently by civil war to realize how much we need the government.

We may not have sworn the oath of loyalty, but by sharing in the privileges of citizenship, by holding a common nationality, and by recognizing natural law, we have a duty to governments as an instrument of God for our good. So we can see why the Preacher should want us to 'obey the king's command'.

Secondly, *he discourages our desire to desert the king* (*verses 3-4*). There may well be decisions and policies over which we wish to protest vigorously, and the most forceful way to do that is to withdraw our support or even engage in disloyal, rebellious action.

But the Preacher has a very down to earth reason for suggesting that you do not rebel. In a few words, it's because you can't win. So what's the use? 'He will do whatever he pleases.' 'A king's word is supreme.' Somehow he always manages to have the last word.

It is still so. You may wish to fight some bureaucratic decision or other but you know that the bureaucrats are clever. They've met it all before. They know how to stall and stonewall and in the end you get nowhere. You may wish to change a policy of central government. But fighting the establishment is to adopt a losing cause. They hold all the trump cards.

It's the same all over the world. In the democratic West it works in a subtle, respectable, socially acceptable way. It pulls the strings through the Official Secrets Acts, through patronage and through its management of the mammoth financial institutions. In dictatorships it works through the silencing of the Press and the banning of opposition. In many other countries it operates through sheer brute force. Whatever the tactic, the end result is the same. The government wins.

That being the case, why take unnecessary risks? You might as well be a part of the system and work on it from the inside, rather than an outcast with no influence at all.

But, thirdly, *he advocates our right to protest against the king* (*verses 5-6*). And that is part of the puzzle and tension of life. The Preacher is not a quietist who says that we are to take everything lying down, no matter what. He is not indifferent to injustice. It is simply that he warns that when misery weighs heavily upon people they need to pick the moment to stand up against injustice and protest with care.

Christians stand in a tradition of freedom-fighters of which they can be proud. From Moses onwards the Bible details one example after another. Moses knew the right method to secure the liberty of the children of Israel from Egypt. Nathan knew the right moment to challenge David. Daniel knew the right way to stand against Nebuchadnezzar. Esther knew the right strategy and was sensitive to the right moment to approach Xerxes and save the Jews from Haman's wicked plots of annihilation. Nehemiah knew the right moment to win the king's approval and lead the Jews back to rebuild Jerusalem. 'But when the time had fully come, God sent his Son, born of a woman, born under law, to redeem those under law, that we might receive the full rights of sons' (Gal. 4:4). Jesus was the greatest freedom fighter of them all.

In subsequent history we stand in the tradition of those who have stood out against oppression: Chrsysostom, Martin Luther, Oliver Cromwell, William Wilberforce, Lord Shaftesbury, Martin Luther King and Desmond Tutu. How is it that the church which has inherited such a tradition of radicalism is able to present itself in such a quietist, conservative light today?

Each of these freedom-fighters knew the time and the way to protest. We need to be equally sensitive to God's timing and God's strategy if we are to enjoy the same sort of success.

Fourthly, *he emphasizes the limitations of the king* (*verses 7-8*). The king may think he has the right to call the tune. The governments of our world seem so powerful with all the military hardware and the financial strings they have at their disposal. Royalty and world leaders look so grand as they strut to their occasions of state in ceremonial robes. But the Preacher says that, like the rest of mankind, in the end they are powerless.

With the persistent thud of the battering-ram on a castle door, he now shatters their pompous authority. No-one can control his own future. No-one has power over his own spirit. No-one has control over the day he is to die. No-one can escape from death: it is as if war has been declared and all have been enlisted for battle. There is no escape. Not even cunning or wickedness will enable a person to wriggle out of death.

So there's a neat enigma. What a riddle! On the one hand, those in authority need to be obeyed, and it pays dividends to be loyal to them. On the other hand, there is a time to rebel against them, and we always need to remember that they are as powerless as the rest of us when it comes to the ultimate authority of death. They are worthy of our respect but should not be idolized. They are worthy of support, but sometimes that support must be withdrawn. They perform superhuman tasks, and yet are as human as the rest of us. They are so much more powerful than we are, and yet they are just as frail as we are. It would be much simpler if such ambiguities didn't exist.

The enigma of death (8:9-10)
The very mention of death leads the Preacher to think of another enigma. There are plenty of questions which surround

death. What does it mean? Why is it so final? What happens afterwards? Is there a future beyond the grave? But there is one particular aspect of it which captures his imagination for the moment, and that is the farce of the funeral.

Admittedly the Hebrew words are difficult to understand, but the Preacher seems to be saying something like this. 'Take a man who has been thoroughly oppressive and wicked. He dies. What happens to him? Well, we give him a great send-off. We take him to church and say nice things about him. We commend him to God's mercy and hint that he's gone to a secure after-life. We don't like to offend at the time of grief. The temple, where he came and went while alive, and which baptized his evil by its complicity, now conspires further to make the unrighteous righteous.'

A few years ago, a vicar hit the headlines in the *Daily Telegraph* for having stated at the funeral of one of his parishioners that he could not think of anything nice to say about him and that no-one would miss him at all. The family and community were up in arms. The bishop was informed. An unspoken code of behaviour had been violated and the vicar was made to apologize. You can't say anything nasty at a funeral!

We find it difficult to admit the reality of divine judgment on a face-to-face basis. When the atheist tyrant Mao Tse-Tung was nearing the end of his life, he was visited by Henry Kissinger, then US Secretary of State, who is a Jew. Mao began to speak about facing God. But Kissinger couldn't handle the conversation and could only joke about it. 'If God calls you, I shouldn't answer if I were you,' said Kissinger. 'The two of you are too big to meet together.'

Mind you, after the farce of the funeral, we soon show what we really think of tyrants, great and small. We soon erase the memory of them. Their policies get reversed, their statues get removed and the streets named after them get new names.

What an enigma! Why is it that we feel we have to be so dishonest in the face of death?

The enigma of injustice (8:11-13)

Injustice isn't reserved for funerals! The Preacher begins to see injustice everywhere. The fact of wickedness is bad enough, but the fact that wickedness never gets its just rewards is even worse. If you are a law-abiding citizen, it seems that you only have to step out of line for a moment and you get pounced on. But rogues get away with persistent wrong-doing and never get caught. It's typical, isn't it? You can be a conscientious driver and never park on a double yellow line. But then, one day, in an emergency, you do so for a short time. The traffic warden is there and pounces. But the neighbour round the corner parks on the double yellow lines all the time and never gets a ticket. How come? There ought to be some iron law which brings the punishment automatically into play. Only then would there be no riddle in law and order.

It's not only that the wicked escape punishment; the Preacher also wants to protest that they enjoy life. They seem to have long lives and a healthy carefree time. While ordinary law-abiding citizens are condemned to face an unending boring routine on the treadmill of work or home, the criminal fraternity are living it up in Rio or Spain, living luxuriously off the proceeds of their latest bank robbery. Nothing upsets us more than such injustice. It's simply not right! It's not fair! If the state can't touch them, why doesn't God punish them? Isn't he interested in right and wrong?

The enigma of misfortune (8:14)

The thought of injustice leads the Preacher progressively into the final riddle he is concerned with here, that of misfortune.

It is bad enough when human beings don't apply justice where they could. But, what is worse, life itself doesn't seem to help. It always seems biased in the wrong direction. Wicked people prosper and live healthily, and righteous people seem burdened and suffer. It's all so unfair! The parcels of retribution and reward have had their labels switched and have been delivered to the wrong addresses. Fortune and misfortune have been reversed and life has conspired to make it so.

As Shakespeare rightly said in *Macbeth*:

> Life's but a walking shadow, a poor player
> that struts and frets his hour upon the stage,
> And then is heard no more: it is a tale
> Told by an idiot, full of sound and fury,
> Signifying nothing.[2]

Or in the more recent words of Ruth Calcin:

> Lord I'm drowning
> In a sea of perplexity
> Waves of confusion crash over me
> I'm too weak to shout for help
> Either quiet the waves
> Or lift me above them
> It's too late to learn to swim.[3]

Perhaps it's too late for you to learn to swim too. Perhaps you are drowning in a sea of perplexity, entangled in the riddles of life, battered by its enigmas and being dragged down by the current of cynicism. So, if you haven't got time to learn to swim, how can the waves be quietened or how can you be lifted above them?

Answers from above

The problem looks worse than it is because the Preacher has been mainly looking at life 'under the sun' (*verses 9, 15*). Consequently he has left half the picture out, or at least not taken the other half of the picture seriously enough. So far we have left that half of the picture out altogether. It's not surprising therefore that neither he nor we can make much sense out of it. Only the full picture can begin to sort out the puzzle.

Without the full picture, life is reduced to a sort of 'Spot the Ball' competition. The object is that you have to plot where the ball is that has been removed from the picture. Is it here, or was it there, or perhaps somewhere else? The point is that the vital piece is missing. Put it back in and it makes perfect sense. It's obvious. Take it out and it's not so obvious at all.

So what is it that he mentions in passing and that we have so far completely omitted? The answer, in a word, is God. Reference is made to four major aspects of God's character and work even while the Preacher is reciting his sorry tale. A secular world that omits God simply does not make sense. But bring these factors into play and, although riddles remain and no-one would claim all the enigmas are solved, you can begin to unravel them. The world starts to make much more sense and you can see possible directions in which the answers lie.

The sovereignty of God (8:2-8)

Rulers like to have the last word and to think they are the last word. But they are not. They think they have the right to the final say about everything. They won't be contradicted. They won't be argued with. They won't listen to lesser mortals.

But underlying all the Preacher's frustrations with rulers is the gleeful thought that they are *not* the final word. God is the last word! One day they will stand in silence before him and will have their deeds reviewed, their policies weighed by one far more significant than any earthly electorate, and their words judged. And so will all of us. God is the one in ultimate control. Earthly rulers operate only in the interim.

The justice of God (8:12-13)

We are frequently puzzled about things until we know the final outcome, and it is the final outcome that matters. That often puts the whole matter in an entirely different light. So it is with the seeming injustice of the world. We cry out for justice. Where is the punishment of those who so blatantly and arrogantly do wrong? Why isn't it on its way? They seem to get away with things easily and live long and happy lives even if they are gross criminals.

But that is not the end of the story. It has been the common conviction of believers, tenaciously held down the centuries, that after death comes judgment (Heb. 9:27). So it is with the Preacher: 'I know that it will go better with God-fearing men, who are reverent before God. Yet because the wicked do not fear God, it will not go well with them, and their days will not lengthen like a shadow.'

In Psalm 73, the writer records his similar struggles with faith. It doesn't seem to pay. The wicked have all the power and fun, and live long lives while the righteous suffer. But the psalmist eventually came to the same conclusion as the Preacher. It certainly looks as if the wicked have the upper hand, but that is a very short-term view. The psalmist describes how he changed his mind when he entered the sanctuary of God and understood the final destiny of the wicked (Ps. 73:17). From the long-term viewpoint it looks very different. Justice will be done and the wicked will receive what they deserve. Rather than being on solid ground, they are, says the psalmist, on a very slippery territory and are sliding down to hell.

The Preacher agrees. The righteous are digging their gardens while the wicked are digging their graves. The cry for justice will one day receive an answer. The answer may not come as quickly as we would like, but it will come none the less.

Just as well, for if there is no judgment then it doesn't matter how you live now. Richard Wurmbrand, a Romanian pastor who suffered years of imprisonment and torture for his faith, has said:

> The cruelty of atheism is hard to believe when man has no faith in the reward of good nor the punishment of evil. There is no reason to be human. There is no restraint from the depths of evil which is in man. The communist torturers often said, 'There is no God, no hereafter, no punishment for evil. We can do what we wish!' I've heard one torturer even say, 'I thank God, in whom I don't believe, that I have lived to this hour when I can express the evil in my heart.' He expressed it in unbelievable brutality and torture inflicted on prisoners.[4]

Wurmbrand is right. But not only is it true that if there is no God you can live how you like. It is also true that, if there is no God and no judgment after this life, then life does not make sense. But if there is, it is an altogether different story.

The gift of God (8:15)

The preacher has not let pessimism take over completely. The puzzles and enigmas are real. Even so it is possible to experience joy and contentment in this life, even if in only a limited manner. The secret lies in seeing what is around you as a gift of God. Food and drink, work and leisure come from him.

They are simple pleasures, but perhaps it is the simple pleasures which are the soundest. Some of our problems arise from our ambition and greed. We have not learned the wisdom of the psalmist who did not concern himself with great matters or things too wonderful for him (Ps. 131:1). Rather was he content with what he had and was grateful for it.

We begin to learn the secret of contentment when we reject the common attitude which thinks in terms of 'my rights'.

When we feel that God, or society, or our families, owe us this or that, we fall into a demanding attitude and are often disappointed and discontented. But once we see that we are owed nothing, then we are free to receive everything we get as a gift and to be grateful for it.

It is vital that we cultivate that spirit of gratitude. The old hymn suggested that we should count our many blessings, name them one by one. But sadly we have got out of that habit and count instead our many complaints. It's not a bad discipline at the end of every day to stop and list things for which we are grateful. It may even be wise, as an aid to discipline, to write them down in a notebook, so that we can be specific in our thinking. Bringing our thanksgiving into sharp focus in that way will soon begin to change our attitudes.

The mysteries of God (8:16-17)
In the end the Preacher has to admit that there are no final answers yet. 'No-one can comprehend what goes on under the sun. Despite all his efforts to search it out, man cannot discover its meaning. Even if a wise man claims he knows, he cannot really comprehend it.'

We can get so far in unravelling the mysteries. Partial answers can be given. Tentative solutions offered. But no-one but an arrogant and unfeeling fool would claim really to understand everything about suffering or injustice or the other enigmas of life. Here we see through a glass darkly. And it will never be any different.

Life under the sun will always be like a jigsaw puzzle with a few bits missing. God has planned it that way so it must be for our good. The missing pieces need not make us unduly anxious, because we know in whose hands they are to be found. And we can trust him. He would give them to us if they were necessary, or if it was for our good.

A boy was being bullied about his father. They said his father put people to sleep and that when they were at his mercy he took out a knife and cut them open and removed their organs or sawed bits off them. It made him sound like a Frankenstein monster! It sounded dreadful. But the boy knew his father and refused to believe he would do such things unless there were a reasonable explanation. Just as well, for the boy's father was in fact a skilled surgeon who had saved many lives by removing cancerous growths from diseased bodies. He saved lives. He was not about destroying life. How you interpret what that man was doing depends on how well you knew him and whether you had reason to trust him or not.

So it is with God. Knowing in whose hands your life rests does not give you cheap answers to every riddle in life, but it does take away the pain of the enigmas and it does quieten the restless waves.

References
1. Quoted by Charles R. Swindoll, *Living on the Ragged Edge* (Word, 1986), p. 236.
2. William Shakespeare, *Macbeth*, V.v.17.
3. Quoted by Swindoll, p. 245.
4. Richard Wurmbrand, *Tortured for Christ* (Hodder & Stoughton, 1967), pp. 34f.

9

HOW TO SQUEEZE THE JUICE OUT OF A LEMON
9:1-18

[1]So I reflected on all this and concluded that the righteous and the wise and what they do are in God's hands, but no man knows whether love or hate awaits him. [2]All share a common destiny – the righteous and the wicked, the good and the bad, the clean and the unclean, those who offer sacrifices and those who do not.

> As it is with the good man,
>   so with the sinner;
> as it is with those who take oaths,
>   so with those who are afraid to take them.

[3]This is the evil in everything that happens under the sun: the same destiny overtakes all. The hearts of men, moreover, are full of evil and there is madness in their hearts while they live, and afterwards they join the dead. [4]Anyone who is among the living has hope – even a live dog is better off than a dead lion!

> [5]For the living know that they will die,
>   but the dead know nothing;
> they have no further reward,
>   and even the memory of them is forgotten.
> [6]Their love, their hate
>   and their jealousy have long since vanished;
> never again will they have a part
>   in anything that happens under the sun.

[7]Go, eat your food with gladness and drink your wine with a joyful heart, for it is now that God favours what you do. [8]Always be clothed in white, and always anoint your head with oil. [9]Enjoy life with your wife, whom you love, all the days of this meaningless life that God has given you under the sun – all your meaningless days. For this is your lot in life and in your toilsome labour under the sun. [10]Whatever your

hand finds to do, do it with all your might, for in the grave, where you are going, there is neither working nor planning nor knowledge nor wisdom.

[11]I have seen something else under the sun:

The race is not to the swift
    or the battle to the strong,
nor does food come to the wise
    or wealth to the brilliant
    or favour to the learned;
but time and chance happen to them all.

[12]Moreover, no man knows when his hour will come:

As fish are caught in a cruel net,
    or birds are taken in a snare,
so men are trapped by evil times
    that fall unexpectedly upon them.

[13]I also saw under the sun this example of wisdom that greatly impressed me: [14]There was once a small city with only a few people in it. And a powerful king came against it, surrounded it and built huge siegeworks against it. [15]Now there lived in that city a man poor but wise, and he saved the city by his wisdom. But nobody remembered that poor man. [16]So I said, "Wisdom is better than strength." But the poor man's wisdom is despised, and his words are no longer heeded.

[17]The quiet words of the wise are more to be heeded
        than the shouts of a ruler of fools.
[18]Wisdom is better than weapons of war,
        but one sinner destroys much good.

What a miserable book Ecclesiastes is! It may be ruthlessly realistic but for many it dwells too much on the emptiness and the problems of life. If you weren't depressed about your life before you began to read the book, you probably are now. If you don't now think that life is just a puff of wind, zilch, nothing, vanity, meaningless, insignificant, chasing after wind, perhaps it is because you have had to distance yourself from its message. Perhaps you could not bear such ruthless honesty.

Its effects reminds me of a story Billy Graham told on one of his visits to Britain. He spoke of a policeman who climbed the Golden Gate Bridge in San Francisco in order to talk down a potential suicide who was about to jump. The policeman told the man that his problems couldn't be that bad and they could all be sorted out in better ways than what he was about to do. Why didn't the man tell him what his problems were? The man began to talk. After twenty minutes both he and the policeman jumped in the river and committed suicide. Sometimes Ecclesiastes can have a similar effect!

If that is the effect it has had on you, you will be glad to know that chapter 9 is something of a turning-point. From now on the Preacher becomes more positive. So stick with it. But before he does so he takes a last lingering look at the frustrations of life and introduces the even greater frustration of death. He tells us in this chapter both how we can crack up and then how we can bear up. The choice is ours.

How to crack up (9:1-6, 12-16)
If you want to crack up, here is how to do so. Spend your time thinking about the two things we all have in common: we face common uncertainties in this life and we face a common destiny in the next. That's a sure recipe for a breakdown or a sure method of inducing paralysis. Let's unpack these two truths.

Our common uncertainties in life
Consider the following four facts.

Tomorrow cannot be known (verse 1)
'No man knows whether love or hate awaits him.' Tomorrow is simply an unopened book as far as we are concerned. We

have our ideas and our plans. We know what we want to do and where we want to go and what we want to achieve, but we cannot be sure of anything. Sudden success might come our way or unexpected opportunities, and suddenly everything is different. Or sudden tragedy might strike us. In a moment the whole of life might be turned upside down. There is no way of knowing.

If we glance ahead to the fact of death which the Preacher will shortly introduce, we have to admit that it is there that uncertainty makes itself known most vividly. In the summer of 1986 the Boston Celtics, America's National Basketball Association champions, signed Len Bias, a twenty-two year old University of Maryland student who stood 6ft 8in tall. He was spoken of as 'America's most brilliant basketball prospect'. Boston was prepared to pay $600,000 for him. He had a thorough physical examination, signed the contract and flew back to Maryland. Within hours he was dead. He was struck down by a heart attack.

It is not an uncommon experience for any minister to find himself at the crematorium with grieving relatives, parting from a loved one who, apparently, had been perfectly healthy a matter of days before. Tomorrow simply cannot be known for sure.

Death is the most dramatic illustration of life's uncertainty but it is far from being the only one. The Preacher hasn't referred to death yet. He simply points out that you cannot tell what reaction you are going to get from people. For no accountable reason they will change – and life will change with them. The New Testament persists in making the same uncomfortable point. 'Now listen, you who say "today or tomorrow we will go to this or that city, spend a year there, carry on business and make money." Why, you do not even know what will happen tomorrow. What is your life? You are a mist that appears for a little while and then vanishes' (Jas. 4:13-14).

Life cannot be safeguarded (verses 2, 12)

He rubs the point in. There are no guarantees in this life. There are no slick formulas. Many people think there ought to be, but the fact is that 'All share a common destiny – the righteous and the wicked, the good and the bad, the clean and the unclean, those who offer sacrifices and those who do not.'

This applies to the Christian as much as to the non-Christian. Becoming a Christian does not exempt you from the ordinary accidents and tragic experiences of life, as some Christians unwisely teach. To listen to some, you would think that being a Christian makes you immune from illness, that financial disaster will never strike, and that you will ever be free from stress. Some seem to give the impression, figuratively speaking, that Christians never need an umbrella. When they walk down the road, though everyone else might get soaked in the rain, they will have a little patch of dryness around them. 'Come to Jesus and all will be perfectly well from that moment on,' they say.

But experience soon teaches a few hard lessons. As Christians we continue to live in a fallen world, and the fallen environment affects us as it does others. Viruses don't distinguish the Christian from the non-Christian. Nor does the rain. Nor does the stock market. Physical death is still experienced by all, and the sense of loss is still experienced by those who remain. We should not be surprised, for the Bible never promises otherwise, and the New Testament teaches much about the suffering that Christians will endure. Being Christians makes many differences and helps us to cope with all those circumstances in a very different way from non-believers. But we share the circumstances in common with everyone else.

It's no good fighting the issue. Just in case we haven't heard what the Preacher is saying, he returns to the theme in verse 12. 'As fish are caught in a cruel net, or birds are taken in a snare, so men are trapped by evil times that fall unexpectedly upon them.' In other words, protest as we might, we are powerless to escape. The same circumstances face us all with the same relentlessness.

Success cannot be guaranteed (verse 11)
Wherever the Preacher looks he is reminded that there is never a guarantee of success. Look to the world of athletics and 'the race is not to the swift'. Look to the world of the army and 'the battle is not to the strong'. Look to the world of good, nice, decent-living people and they don't always have enough food. Look to the world of the university and they certainly don't make a lot of money nor do they always experience favourable circumstances.

Why not? Because 'time and chance could happen to them all'. It's true, isn't it? Would some of our great athletes be what they are, had some of their opponents not suffered unfortunately from injury? Would England's success in football have been much greater if Gazza had not been so frequently injured? Is Rusedski the best tennis player in the UK, or is it just that he had the right coach and the right opportunities at the right moment, and others had not?

Or take the world of politics. Would Churchill have been acknowledged as the great prime minister he was, had he not been called to govern during the war? Was it those dreadful circumstances that enhanced his greatness, and during peace would he have passed unnoticed? Would Anthony Eden have been a much greater prime minister but for the slip of a surgeon's knife? Would Harold Wilson have been prime minister at all apart from the unexpected death of Hugh Gaitskell?

Or take war. We all think that the battles are won by the brilliant strategy of the generals. In reality, at least until the present age of war, the vanquishing of enemy armies has had much more to do with the weather or with illness than with brilliant military opponents.

Or take science. All the hard work cannot be discounted. But many of the great discoveries have been made apparently by accident.

Or take musicians. Why do some make it to the top and get into the charts, whereas others, with equal talent, pass unnoticed? So much depends on someone 'discovering' them just at the right moment and signing them up with the right management and contracts.

So much depends apparently on 'time and chance'.

People cannot be trusted (verses 13-16)

The Preacher speaks of the fourth uncertainty we face in life by telling a touching story. Some of the details are obscure, and different translations treat it differently, all with equal reason. What is clear is that a small city is under siege by a powerful army. And in that city is a poor but wise man. What is not clear is whether they turned to him and listened and took the action he suggested, so saving the city, and then forgot him. That is how the NIV and RSV translate it. Or, as the GNB interprets it, perhaps they forgot he was there all along and, rather than turning to him at the crucial moment and saving themselves, they forgot him and so the city fell. Either way, the point is that they refused to remember this poor but wise man just when they needed to do so, either to express their gratitude or to follow his leadership.

People are fickle. They don't act in a consistent and rational way. You can perform some great act of kindness or service, and those who have benefited will soon forget. Rather than expressing gratitude they will take it for granted. And it hurts. Or you can be all ready and qualified to do something of great benefit, but because your face doesn't fit they don't want to know. They don't even think about you. How stupid is such pride. You can never be sure of either your path or your treatment in life. We all share the same uncertainties.

Our common destiny in the next life
As if that isn't enough to render us quivering wrecks, the Preacher now turns his attention to something else we all have in common – our destiny in death. The Preacher has three things to say about it.

Death is all-embracing (verse 3)
The Times ran an advert for an investment company on several occasions one summer. It carried the headline 'Whether you die or whether you don't ...'. It seems to have escaped the notice of the advertisers that we all will die and that such a statement is nonsense. That certainly is the thought preoccupying the Preacher. 'The same destiny overtakes all.' Charles De Gaulle once said, 'Stalin said only one serious thing to me, "In the end death is the only winner."' It is the great leveller. 'We all fall down.' It makes little difference then whether we were great or small in this world. We all go the same way.

Death is evil (verse 3)
Death continues the evil that people have practised in life. It is an absurdity, a madness. We want to protest at it. What a waste! Why is it so final? Why does it render so much of life absurd? Have you ever thought how utterly foolish death makes the world look? On the one hand we spend millions of pounds on the Health Service trying to stave it off and postpone its arrival. On the other hand we spend even more millions of pounds developing bombs and buying military hardware in order to kill people. What an ambivalent attitude we have to it. It's OK, providing it happens to someone else – preferably at the other side of the world from us. What fools it makes us look!

Death is empty (verses 5-6)

What does the Preacher think happens after death? Nothing much, according to verses 5 and 6 (although he is more positive in 12:7). Here he voices the commonly accepted view of the Old Testament about the after-world. Those who died, according to the Old Testament teaching, went to Sheol where they carried on existing in a very unreal, shadowy, insubstantial sort of way. It wasn't extinction. But it might just as well have been. All that you could really say about it you had to say on negative terms. Those who lived there were characterized by having no knowledge, no reward, no memory, no emotions and no significance. Elsewhere the picture painted is one where there is no light, no joy, no praise, no noise and no conversation. Everything is nothing, nothing, nothing.

Now the Christian doesn't see the afterlife like that at all any more. Christ has opened that way to us to a new understanding by his resurrection from the dead. The New Testament teaches that his followers are going to a place where life will be at its richest and fullest. There will be praise, joy, recognition and significance there. The only things which will be absent will be the negative things like pain, tears and sorrow. The revelation of God's truth has moved on since Ecclesiastes was written.

But the hopelessness of the Preacher is still widely shared by the unbeliever. Some form of life after death is commonly accepted but very vague. There's not much to look forward to in such folk-religious views. Death is widely seen as a tragedy because the words of Christ about the future are not really believed. What matters most is this life – not the next.

The Preacher voices what most really still believe. 'While there's life, there's hope', we say. He says, 'Even a live dog is better off than a dead lion.' Since dogs were despised as unclean and unhealthy and the lion was considered to be the noblest of beasts, the king of the jungle, he is making a startling claim. The contrast has even more point. Hope, apparently belongs only to this life and it is better to have that than anything. It is certainly better to be barely alive and despised than nobly esteemed and dead.

What with the uncertainties we share in this life and the destiny we share in the next, why don't we all crack up?

How to bear up

At long last the Preacher begins to be more positive. It's a trend which becomes even more noticeable as the book wends its way to its conclusion. But here he just begins to relax a little.

The answers do not lie where most people think they do. Materialism doesn't help. We brought nothing into the world and we take nothing out. Materialism only heightens our sense of the absurd in the light of the grave. Nor is the answer to be found in resignation. That implies that God is a cosmic sadist determined to make sure that you only just survive the experience of life! Nor does the answer lie in reckless hedonism. Pleasure at all costs, regardless of any moral rules, doesn't help, since life is at least in some measure a preparation for death. So what is the answer?

The answer is to live life to the full now, seeing it as a gift from God. Many people never do so. They let life pass them by while they are waiting for it to begin. But life is too short to postpone enjoyment until an indefinite tomorrow. Benjamin Disraeli understood it when he said, 'Life is too short to be small.' And the saintly Andrew Murray meant the same thing when he said, 'Life must be filled with life.'

So how do you go about living in the 'now'? The secret, in part, at least, according to the Preacher, lies in being free enough in your mind to enjoy four different things.

Enjoy contentment (9:7)

The first area is one which he has mentioned before (5:18-20; 8:15). Food and wine are seen as basic gifts of God, but they also conjure up the picture of life which is well provided for and satisfying. There's nothing like a good meal as a way to enjoy yourself or to celebrate.

So the Preacher asks us to consider why it is that we have been given the means to enjoy ourselves by God and still do not do so. What do we need that we do not already have before enjoyment can begin? What's missing? Isn't there sufficient to begin looking positively on life already? There certainly is. So there is no point in postponing the enjoyment. 'It is now that God favours you.'

So let's get on with life today in a positive frame of mind. Life will be ruined if we indefinitely postpone its start. Many of us do, of course. We think things will be different when we've left home, when we've left college, when we're married, when we have a new job, or any job at all, when we've got promotion, when we've moved to a new house, when the children have grown up, and so on and so on. But will life really begin then any more than it can now? Tomorrow, in that sense, never comes.

Some people ruin life in a serious way by this indefinite postponement syndrome. I think of a lady who was convinced she was going to marry a certain person. Much to everyone else's frustration, she refused to get a job or make any plans for herself, expecting her Prince Charming to propose shortly. He was oblivious of her desires and had no plans to reciprocate her love. But she persisted and lived in limbo for two years as a result. If only she had taken God's 'now' seriously.

Take today as a gift from God. Take your present circumstances as a gift from God. Take your job, your study, your home, your family, as a gift from God. Enjoy them now and use them to the full. Reject the indefinite postponement syndrome.

Enjoy comfort (9:8)
Verse 8 may not make much sense to us. We may not always want to be clothed in white. We may think that if we were to do so we would just make a lot of washing! And we may certainly not want to anoint our heads with oil! It's messy! But the original readers would have understood the Preacher. In a hot climate, wearing white made a good deal of sense because it reflected the heat and kept you cool. Anointing with oil made you feel good too, just as a bubble bath or the use of certain cosmetics does today.

He is, therefore, advocating that you enjoy the comforts which God has provided for you. He does not advocate selfish pleasure-seeking. He is merely recommending that you make sensible use of the comforts God has provided your society with. In other words, it isn't more spiritual to be a masochist. You don't necessarily become more holy and satisfied in life by being an ascetic. In rejecting the gifts of God you may well be rejecting the giver as well. Rather, as Paul tells Timothy, 'everything God created is good, and nothing is to be rejected if it is received with thanksgiving, because it is consecrated by the word of God and prayer' (1 Tim. 4:4-5). Harold Kushner points out that the Talmud, the collected wisdom of the Rabbis, has a relevant saying, 'In the world to come, each of us will be called to account for all the good things God put on earth which we refused to enjoy.'[1]

So take what God gives. Take the comforts he has provided and don't feel guilty about enjoying them. Don't be afraid to believe in a colourful God who invented a world of lovely things that we, as his children, can enjoy. Don't live imprisoned by fear and guilt, condemned perpetually by an over-sensitive conscience. Where God gives, receive with thankfulness. The thankfulness will keep you humble and will free you from selfishness. It will remind you that all that you have is a gift from God and that it is not yours of right. It will remind you of the needs of others. But not to receive what God has provided is a slight on him and an unnecessary infliction on yourself.

Enjoy companionship (9:9)

I am not sure that I would have wanted the Preacher to preach at my wedding! When you read the first half of the verse 9 you may think of it as a lovely wedding address. 'Enjoy life with your wife, whom you love....' But then he ruins it. His cynicism peeps through as he adds, '... all the days of this meaningless life ... all your meaningless days.'

We might wish that he was capable of being more romantic and that his sentimentality was unalloyed. But a moment's reflection convinces you that he is right, particularly as he is writing about the godless perspective, life 'under the sun'. Marriage is not a blissful cocoon that protects the happy couple from the enigmas of life or the problems of the world. Indeed marriage brings hurt and pain in its train which would never have been experienced if the couple had stayed single. If the marriage blots out the needs of others and swings from one blissful cloud-nine moment to another, it is probably a sign that the marriage is too self-centred and introverted. So, the Preacher is right. The backcloth even of a happy marriage remains 'this meaningless life'.

His advice, however, is that you should not concentrate on the backcloth at the expense of the foreground. Many make that mistake. It's true that there are lots of problems which will never be resolved. But that should not stop us from enjoying the good things which are ready to hand. God has given us the beauty and joy of human love. He made us to fall head over heels, to be off our food, to float on cloud-nine when we fall in love. The romance needs to be kept alive and the love, ever in danger of growing old and tired, needs to be kept aflame. So buy the flowers, send the cards, find new ways of saying 'I love you' every day. Be spontaneous. Spend time doing things together and whispering sweet nothings to each other. Enjoy each other.

Stephen Travis tells us of a divorce-court judge who accepted that a marriage had irretrievably broken down when the husband complained that for the last ten years his wife had never given him anything else for Christmas or birthdays other than a pair of socks and some handkerchiefs.[2] All the spontaneity, the vitality, the enjoyment, had settled into a dull routine. But it need not happen that way. Admittedly it takes thought and work, rather than just taking each other for granted. But it's worth it.

Perhaps, too, the Preacher's reference to 'the wife of your youth' is a means of emphasizing that you are to enjoy life now. Some marriages go sour because the partners think that they can only begin to enjoy each other some time in the future – when there is more money in the bank, or the home of their dreams has been purchased, or the children have arrived. But no! Right from the beginning even youthful marriages can be full of enjoyment.

Others go wrong because they think the time of enjoyment was in the past. That sort of thing all belonged to their youthful days and they are no longer young. But no! The wife, or husband, you had when you were young can still be enjoyed into old age. Of course many changes will have taken place. The wife may no longer be the stunning physical beauty she was as the wear and tear of the years and the family have taken their toll. The husband may not be the handsome go-getter that he was. Indeed, he may never have fulfilled the potential the wife thought he had, or he might now be on the downward slope. But no matter, enjoyment can still be rich and companionship sweet if the partners go on giving themselves for each other (Eph. 5:21-33).

So, whether the relationship is new or old, keep the romance alive and enjoy each other today. I'm not sure it's the wisest way to put it because honeymoons can be difficult and stressful times. But given the popular idea of honeymoons I'm sure the Preacher is inviting married couples to enjoy one lifelong honeymoon.

Enjoy confidence (9:10)

In contrast to Sheol, life here should be active, energetic, practical, informed and skilful. Life is what you make of it. You have plenty of opportunities. You can either just sit and stare at them or you can set to and use them. You can go through life as if suffering from premature senility if you wish to do so. You can be a fully paid-up member of the old people's home at the age of thirty if you choose. But if you do that, it is because you choose it, not because that is how God made you. You can be diffident and uncertain about everything, if that is what you want.

I know one fellow who takes half an hour to acknowledge your cheery 'Good morning'. He takes that long because he spends a quarter of an hour working out whether it is morning or not and then another fifteen minutes calculating whether it is good or not! He's diffident in the extreme and painful to know. But the choice is his.

In this life God has given us energy, work, mental abilities, knowledge and wisdom. Let us use them! If we don't use them here, it is certain that we won't get the opportunity to use them in the hereafter. Our confidence need not rest in ourselves but in the God who gave them to us. To deny that we have them is to call God a liar. We can be confident, because we trust in him. In using them we will find that 'God favours' what we do.

All this enjoyment stems from our acceptance by God (*verse 7*). The believer need not struggle restlessly for acceptance, since through Jesus Christ he is already accepted by God. Nothing he can do can make him more or less accepted. Christ has done it all. That being so, what the believer can do is to relax and enjoy himself. He can stop striving and having to prove himself. He can stop anxiously looking over his shoulder and wondering. He can be free to get on with life and enjoy it to the full.

So how do we squeeze the juice out of a lemon? The answer is 'With all your might'. Get all the juice out of it that you can, not just a pathetic dribble. And do the same with your life. The choice before us all is to concentrate our thinking either on the things that will make us crack up or on the things that will help us to bear up. The Preacher invites us to be positive. We can get so much out of life now, if we want to do so.

References
1. Harold Kushner, *When All You Ever Wanted Isn't Enough* (Pan, 1987), p. 82.
2. Stephen Travis, *I Believe in the Second Coming* (Hodder & Stoughton, 1982), p. 214.

10

THE ANATOMY OF FOLLY
10:1-20

[1]As dead flies give perfume a bad smell,
   so a little folly outweighs wisdom and honour.
[2]The heart of the wise inclines to the right,
   but the heart of the fool to the left.
[3]Even as he walks along the road,
   The fool lacks sense
   and shows everyone how stupid he is.
[4]If a ruler's anger rises against you,
   do not leave your post;
   calmness can lay great errors to rest.

[5]There is an evil I have seen under the sun,
   the sort of error that arises from a ruler:
[6]Fools are put in many high positions,
   while the rich occupy the low ones.
[7]I have seen slaves on horseback,
   while princes go on foot like slaves.

[8]Whoever digs a pit may fall into it;
   whoever breaks through a wall may be bitten by a snake.
[9]Whoever quarries stones may be injured by them;
   whoever splits logs may be endangered by them.

[10]If the axe is dull
   and its edge unsharpened,
more strength is needed
   but skill will bring success.

[11]If a snake bites before it is charmed,
     there is no profit for the charmer.

[12]Words from a wise man's mouth are gracious,
   but a fool is consumed by his own lips.

[13]At the beginning his words are folly;
    at the end they are wicked madness –
    [14]and the fool multiplies words.

No-one knows what is coming –
    who can tell him what will happen after him?

[15]A fool's work wearies him;
    he does not know the way to town.

[16]Woe to you, O land whose king was a servant
    and whose princes feast in the morning.
[17]Blessed are you, O land whose king is of noble birth
    and whose princes eat at a proper time –
    for strength and not for drunkenness.

[18]If a man is lazy, the rafters sag;
    if his hands are idle, the house leaks.

[19]A feast is made for laughter,
    and wine makes life merry,
    but money is the answer for everything.

[20]Do not revile the king even in your thoughts,
    or curse the rich in your bedroom,
because a bird of the air may carry your words,
    and a bird on the wing may report what you say.

There are weeks when I think I am surrounded by fools! I
realise that it isn't recommended for me to say that too often
or too loudly, but it's true. I also realize that Jesus said that
we should not call anyone a fool or else we would be in danger of hell fire (Matt. 5:22). So let me explain.

When Jesus talked of calling someone a fool, he was using a term which meant 'a worthless person'. I'm using the
word 'fool' with the meaning which the Old Testament gives
to it – someone who is unwise. It's easy to see why so much
of the Old Testament, which provides us with acute observations on life, should harp on the theme of wisdom and folly.

Some people have little going for them and yet get much from life because they live wisely. They may not have money, education, status or even health – but they have wisdom. And that is to be prized above all. Others have everything going for them but ruin it all because they are fools. They make the wrong choices, they lack discernment and discretion, and everything they do to get out of the mess they create just makes it worse.

There are times when I think I am surrounded by fools because I know so many people who keep making the wrong choices, who ruin good friendships and relationships, who cut people dead who long to help them, who fritter away money they desperately need for basics and who show no understanding at all about building relationships.

In a nutshell, fools show no understanding of responsibility. Bernard Levin, who often wrote about fools, wrote a piece in *The Times* on 27 June 1983 on 'Relative Values'.[1] It spoke of the problem being faced by the councillors of Copeland in Cumbria, where half of the Council's housing tenants had failed to pay their rent. Naturally that left the Council with a huge difficulty in meeting its own bills. When enquiries were made as to why people could not afford to pay, the Council learned that its tenants held some interesting attitudes. One family could not afford to pay, although the breadwinner was earning £7,500 a year, because they were paying £25 a week to hire five television sets and three video recorders. Another family could not pay because of the cost of their holiday to Algeria, which they had taken only because on their holiday in Malta, earlier in the year, it had rained all the time.

The books we know in the Old Testament as wisdom literature, especially the book of Proverbs, would have no difficulty in calling such people fools. They've no idea of priorities or of responsibilities, and simply can't, or won't, work their lives out in a sensible way.

The relentless realism of Ecclesiastes, which is part of that wisdom literature, confronts the issue. It would be surprising if it did not. As you look at the world you see people who are wise and people who are fools. Perhaps we ought to say, however, that the teaching of these books is only one perspective on the matter. What it says is true, but not the whole truth. Its down-to-earth common sense is refreshingly honest. Its blunt speaking is appealing. But there is more that could be said. We should not write the fool off because of what we read. He is capable of redirecting his life, of being born again, in the mercy of God, just as anyone else is. And if there are times when I think I am surrounded by fools, praise God that I can also count many converted fools among my friends.

But what does the author mean by 'fool'?

Fools in general (10:1-4)
Before dealing with specific issues, the Preacher gives us a bird's-eye view of folly and points out some of its most prominent characteristics.

It doesn't take much ...(10:1)
... to be a fool. It doesn't take much to ruin a whole batch of perfume. Just one little fly, that's all, and the lot is useless. Where ever you look you see visual aids pointing to the same lesson. A little chemical spillage can pollute a whole river. One bad ingredient in cooking will ruin a whole batch of food. One tiny loose nut (not the driver), and the whole complex mechanism of a car engine can come grinding to a halt. I know, it's happened to me.

So it is with folly. A person may have a great deal of wisdom and achieve many positive things, and a single wrong choice will ruin it all. A politician has an affair and his promising career is brought to an abrupt end. A civil servant compromises security and he's out on his neck, if not in prison. A policeman hides the truth about one case, and he's called to account. A gambler loses his fortune in a single night. A young lad gets involved in one petty crime and gets dragged down a path into more and more crime from which he can't escape. Ask John Profumo, Richard Nixon, Edward Kennedy or Jonathan Aitken and you will soon see what I mean.

It inclines to the left (10:2)

This verse, much loved by Conservative politicians, needs some explaining. It has nothing to do with one's political views even though I heard a member of John Major's administration quote it (in jest, I think!). What is more, it is based on dubious anatomy. The heart is not on the right. But the Hebrews associated the right with being skilful and resourceful and they associated the left with disfavour. The link still persists in popular imagination. Parents still feel a little uneasy when they discover their child to be left-handed, and we still regard the left as sinister. At the same time we use the word 'dexterity', which originally had to do with being right-handed, for skill in handling things.

What has all that got to do with folly and wisdom? Just this. The heart is the invisible side of life. It is the seat of motivation. If our motives are warped and we are spiritually incompetent then we are heading for trouble. Being wise has to do with being right on the inside.

It soon shows (10:3)

Fools stick out like sore thumbs. They only have to walk down the road and they show themselves for what they are for all to see. The statement provokes a ready response in us. We have all seen people who draw attention to themselves by their dress and behaviour. They think they are the latest word in fashion, but really they are saying far more about themselves than anything else. Rowdiness, drunkenness, dare-devil games with cars, walking across car bonnets, and so on, are all conjured up by what he says.

Even when the folly is not on display for the public enjoyment, it soon becomes evident. The fool only has to open his mouth and you know it. It is difficult for a fool to help himself.

It shows most ... (10:4)
... in the huff! That's Derek Kidner's helpful explanation of this verse. 'What we are being invited to notice is that absurd human phenomenon, the huff!'[2] It happens to us all sooner or later. The boss expresses his disapproval of us, and there are two ways we can react to it. We can react foolishly, throw up our post, bear a grudge, demand an apology, feel all hurt and blow a fuse. Or we can handle it wisely. We can examine the issue, see if there was any justice in what was said, and see what we can learn from it. If we genuinely can't find any reason for his anger, we can rationalize it. Perhaps the boss is having a rough time at home or his car broke down on the way to work! That will help us to react with calmness and not to exacerbate the situation. The RSV puts it like this: 'Deference will make amends for great offences.' Such advice may not be popular today, since most people are very keen on demanding their own rights and being on the same level with their bosses. But popular or not, it remains practical.

Folly in high places (10:5-7, 16-17)
We're told by those who know that the popular television programmes *Yes, Minister* and *Yes Prime Minister* accurately portrayed life at the top. If so, there seems a great deal of folly around in the high echelons of government. Folly is not confined to the lower social classes! The subtlety of these

programmes lies in the fact that you're never quite clear who the fool is. Is it the bumbling politician Jim Hacker, or the devious, scheming civil servant, Sir Humphrey Appleby, who, for all his erudition, gets outwitted quite often? They're both as bad as each other.

Obviously fools in government is no new phenomenon. They can be traced back through history. In our own day we have had Pol Pot and Saddam Hussein. They show that fools can be dangerous. Others are more to be pitied. George III used to address trees in Windsor Great Park. The Roman Emperor Caligula proposed that his horse be elected a consul and kitted him out with a marble stall and purple blankets. Both of these may have been a little mad. Many more have behaved in a foolish and irresponsible way without the benefit of that justification. It seems as if the Preacher was aware of folly in high places in his day!

The Preacher puts down the presence of folly in high places to one simple cause. The wrong people have got into government. They are the wrong people because, in the natural order of things, they were never meant to govern. They don't have the right background, the right breeding, or the right old-school tie to be leaders. According to him, when slaves ride on horseback and servants become kings then you can expect trouble. It's wrong because it's unnatural. The Preacher regards it as natural that the princes and the rich should govern. Only when what is natural is put into practice will wisdom thrive.

We democrats may not like what he is saying, but we must remember that he probably uncritically accepted the views of the circles in which he moved. We ought not to judge him from the very different perspective of our own time. It is always difficult to see our own prejudices and assumptions, because they are so much a part of us. We are often totally oblivious to them. We may think that democracy is right and that our system must be open enough for anyone to rise through the ranks to power. But we'd be hard pushed to justify it from the Bible as the only legitimate way to govern, and we'd be hard pushed to prove that democracy has always guaranteed wise leadership.

We need to remember too that until recently many people would have thought the same as the Preacher. When I first studied sociology it was still possible to identify the deferential manual worker. They were people who worked in the old heavy industries and doffed their caps to their masters, thought they were their betters, and voted Conservative in elections because they thought the aristocracy, or at least the upper middle classes, were the natural party of government. They accepted paternalism reasonably happily and were anything but revolutionary. So perhaps he's not all that out of date.

What is more, like it or not, we all have at least a remnant of such views within us. Robert Davidson has updated the picture, and perhaps in doing so catches us out and reveals our own prejudices. He says that today the Preacher would talk about a man driving a Rolls Royce to the Social Security office to collect his unemployment benefit, while a man who moves among the social elite doesn't have the fare to take a taxi home.[3] We'd think there was something unnatural about that, wouldn't we?

Having tried to bracket the objections which might come into our minds as we read this text, let's now try and understand the Preacher's concern. Why does he think it's such a bad idea for those from the lower social orders to rule?

Essentially, he says, they are not equipped to handle it. They are likely to abuse their power and take away the dignity of others. So they are likely to make princes walk while they ride in style. They are also likely to abuse their power by having a jolly good time themselves instead of getting on with the serious business of government. They are likely to have drink-sodden dinners which reach into the next morning and leave them quite incapable of functioning as the government next day. The picture conjures up King John and the Sheriff of Nottingham, of Robin Hood fame. The TV serials always show them as villains making just those mistakes. They engage in a continuous round of drunken orgies which leave them unfit to rule. The result is that their decisions are unjust, take away the rights and dignity of their subjects, and leave the state vulnerable to its enemies.

Perhaps the Preacher has a point after all. In our media-infested age it is difficult to know the truth about the private lives of our public leaders. But I have no doubt that their private behaviour and personal characters are relevant to whether they make fit rulers or not. If they are not capable of making right and disciplined choices in their own lives, and of managing their own families, why should we trust them with wider responsibilities? No doubt there are still fools in government, and every now and again the newspapers justly expose one or the courts justly call one to account. Then the value of the Preacher's words can be seen. The land which has such rulers is in a sorry condition, while the land where rulers are fit to govern is blessed indeed.

Before we leave these verses, another possible interpretation of verses 5-7 should be acknowledged. Because the words which the Preacher uses for 'ruling' in these verses are unusual, some have thought that the Preacher is talking of higher authorities than earthly ones. Some apply these verses to God and the devil. Then the meaning becomes something like this. It is a real evil when the Devil usurps the authority of God. When he does so things get turned upside-down and God's wise design in creation gets ruined. That is certainly true.

Paul talks in Romans 1 of the way in which we call 'right' 'wrong' when the Devil is in control. Again, in 1 Corinthians 1 he speaks of the foolishness of going after what we think is wisdom, while rejecting God's way.

We cannot be dogmatic about which interpretation is correct. Either way, the Preacher pleads for one essential thing – that we don't let fools usurp the power authority of those who are truly wise.

Fools lack balance (10:8-11)

The common thread in these baffling verses is the need for balance. Verses 8 and 9 talk of the need for the wise person to find a middle path between reckless indiscretion and unadventurous inhibition. Verses 10 and 11 talk of the need for the wise person to find a middle path between haste and over-cautious procrastination.

It seems that the intent of the person who digs a pit or breaks through a wall is malicious. He digs a pit as a trap for someone else to fall into. He breaks through a wall as an act of criminal damage to a neighbour's property. But the person who perpetrates either of these wilful acts is likely to meet his come-uppance. He might well be digging his own grave or he might well meet unexpected danger through the wall. As the old proverb says, 'If you play with fire you must expect to get burnt.'

It is more likely that such a sensible warning will be misinterpreted by some people. They will get it out of all proportion and seize on it as a reason for never doing anything of an active or adventurous sort. Already fearful that all activity involves some risk, they will use the Preacher's words to justify their inhibitions. So the Preacher balances what he has said. In verse 9 he speaks of activity which is not only legitimate but which serves a good and useful purpose. He admits that this activity, like most worthwhile activity, involves an element of risk. But the unspoken implication is that in spite of that you must still engage in it.

So a balance must be found. The fool is reckless and invites trouble by his behaviour. The wise person will live sensibly and not go looking for trouble. But he must accept that trouble is a fact of life, and even when he is not looking for it it's likely to strike. Retreating into the safety of a cotton-wool existence where you obsessively try to avoid trouble is just another form of foolishness. Wisdom picks its way through both extremes.

The next two pictures show us two other forms of folly. They speak of opposite extremes in our use of time. In verse 10 we have a picture of impetuous haste. The person is so quick to get on with the job that he actually makes it more difficult for himself by failing to invest a little time in wise preparation first. If only he had stopped to sharpen the axe before he used it he might well have found that it was much easier to chop the tree down. The job would have been completed in half the time. Rushing in without thought and preparation is often characteristic of fools. The relevance of this picture has increased in the age of instant everything. People want to lead churches or evangelize the world without training first. They want to go and live overseas without learning the language. They want to get married and have a family without saving up. Often this undue haste can rapidly lead to failure and disappointment. Time spent in preparation is worth it.

On the other hand there are some people who spend so long in preparing themselves that they never actually do the job for which they are preparing. And they are equally foolish. Verse 11 presents us with a comic sight. The snake gets impatient waiting for the charmer to summon him out of the basket so he pops up of his own accord and bites a passer-by. Hardly a way for a snake-charmer to make a successful living! He committed the sin of procrastination.

Many people do the same. Some students never hand in essays on time because they are sure there is just one more book or article that they must read. Some people never get into full-time Christian work because there is one more course with which they must equip themselves. People never accept the chances offered because they are fearful that the time is not just right.

Again balance is needed. We need to prepare ourselves wisely, but not so that we waste years when we could actually be practising. The wise person shows discernment. Wisdom will lead us through the middle path. Preparation, yes, but not too much.

Fools and their tongues (10:12-14, 20)

Our tongues cause us more trouble than most other parts of our bodies! We can detect wisdom or folly there more easily than virtually anywhere else in our lives. Wisdom literature was full of advice about what we say and how we say it. Look at some of the sensible advice the book of Proverbs gives about the matter. It deals with it in 10:14, 20, 32; 12:14, 18-19, 25; 17:28; 18:21; 21:23; 25:11-12, and in many other places. It would be a serious omission if the Preacher didn't say something about the matter.

It's not just an Old Testament issue. On into the New Testament James returns to it. All James says in 3:1-12 confirms the continuing importance of what the Old Testament has taught. He is very much the New Testament wisdom writer, and significantly he immediately links what he says about the tongue to the need for wisdom. Christians need to learn some practical lessons about their words and not be too heavenly minded in thinking that their lips will just look after themselves.

What does the Preacher have to say about the matter?

A fool's words are destructive (10:12)
In the end a fool's words destroy him. But in the process of doing so they destroy other people because they are insensitive, wounding, arrogant and deceptive. In contrast, the words of a wise person will be gracious. They will bring healing and they will build up the person to whom they are addressed. Proverbs tells us that wise words are like apples of gold in a setting of silver (25:11). Paul tells us that we are not to let 'any unwholesome talk come out of our mouths, but only what is helpful for building others up according to their needs' (Eph. 4:29).

A fool's words are plenty (10:14)
A fool's words multiply and there's no stopping them. What is more, they get worse as they go on. The more the fool talks the more he likes the sound of his own voice. The more he talks the more expansive he gets in his claims. The more he tries to get out of what he has said before, the worse mess he gets himself into.

Again we're in the world of *Yes, Prime Minister*. It seems that some are deliberately trained to cultivate the art of spinning together words which sound impressive but actually say nothing. Virtually every conversation in those television programmes would serve to illustrate the Preacher's point. How about this, not from Sir Humphrey but from one of his colleagues. He was writing to the Prime Minister.

When I said that HA was not overstretched, I was of course talking in the sense of total cumulative loading taken globally rather than in respect of certain individual and essentially anomalous responsibilities which are not, logically speaking, consonant or harmonious with the broad spectrum of intermeshing and inseparable functions and could indeed be said to be an excessive and superrogatory burden on the office when considered in relation to the comparatively exiguous advantages of their overall consideration.[5]

Enough said!

A fool's words are ignorant (10:14)
A journalist once asked Churchill what were the necessary qualifications of a politician. The great man put on his bulldog look and replied, 'It is the ability to foretell what is going to happen tomorrow, next week, next month and next year.' (Pause) 'And to have the ability afterwards to explain why it didn't happen.'[6] How that squares with what the Preacher says about fools I will leave it to the reader to work out.

According to the Preacher, the fool doesn't know the future with any certainty, for no-one can. But that doesn't stop him talking about it with great confidence or even a fair degree of arrogance. When his predictions have been proved false by events (as, of course, they will), he either refuses to admit that he said what he did say, or lets forth another torrent of words to explain why he was wrong. It would have been better for him to say nothing in the first place.

The wise person humbly admits what he does not know and listens to the opinion of others.

A fool's words are dangerous (10:20)
The fool's lack of discretion is liable to lead him into all sorts of trouble. Because he can't control his tongue, his innermost thoughts are bound to seep out and be reported to higher authorities and land him in trouble.

We have a saying that 'even the walls have ears'. A variation on the theme brought the matter home to me even more on a trip to Romania before the Revolution. We met a man on a tram who, hearing my wife and I speak English, engaged us in conversation. He said he would be viewed with some suspicion for talking to foreigners but he wouldn't miss an opportunity to practise his English. As he showed us around his city he looked at some concrete buildings and said, 'Do you know what they say here about the way we make concrete? We make it 20% sand, 20% pebbles, 10% cement and 50% Secret Service microphones.' For some in our world it is literally true that the walls have ears. But even where it is not literally true, the saying, together with the Preacher, reminds us that our words have a way of boomeranging on us and knocking us flat.

Fools: life's just too much for them (10:15, 18)
The Preacher provides us with only a passing glance of a very familiar image of the fool which we find in the book of Proverbs. There we regularly meet the tragic yet comic figure of the sluggard. He's hinged to his bed (26:14). When he does get up he's too lazy to lift his spoon to put his cornflakes in his mouth (26:15). Any excuse is good enough to stop him actually doing anything (26:13). Consequently he dies of unfulfilled ambition (13:4; 21:25), proves a pain in the neck to everyone else (10:26), and is constantly unprepared for his future and so limps from crisis to crisis (24:30-34). Even silly little ants could teach him a thing or two (6:6-11). For all the humour of this picture, the sluggard is morally culpable, for 'one who is slack in his work is brother to one who destroys' (18:9).[7]

The few brush-strokes of the Preacher in Ecclesiastes give us enough to discern the main outlines of the fool. At root his problem is one of sheer laziness. His work wearies him. That results in his total incompetence. He doesn't know the way to town. That shows how sad a figure he is. Everyone else knows the way to town. It's basic information available to all. If he really didn't know the way, all he had to do was ask. But not him! Perhaps he doesn't really want to know the way. Such an approach to life ends in ruin. His rafters sag, his roof leaks, and unless he changes his way of life drastically the whole thing is going to cave in on him.

Some fools are quite likeable. The *Book of Heroic Failures*[8] is full of them. Criminals who can't pull off their crime because they are too plain stupid; politicians and others who lose votes when everyone's on their side; firemen who drive their engines over cats they've just rescued from trees; brides who marry the wrong man; gunners who shoot the wrong targets, and so on. Fools can provide great entertainment.

At the same time there is a serious side to folly. It can carry with it tremendous spiritual liabilities. Be a fool if you want to be. But first count the cost. It is likely that if you act the fool you will ruin your life. The burden of Ecclesiastes is that there are enough things conspiring to do that for you already. They don't need your help. Furthermore, being a fool in this life is a rotten preparation for the next life. The essence of being a fool is that you have not taken God, or his words, seriously (Prov. 1:7). So it's not a good wicket on which to bat if you want to be acceptable to him in eternity.

No-one need be a fool. God's wisdom can save us from folly. If we reject the Devil's usurped authority in our lives and place ourselves under the control of Jesus Christ, then he can give us his protection from mistakes, provide us with balance, help us to master our tongues and give us his own life and energy. That will get us moving in the direction of building a life which is pleasing to him.

References

1. Reproduced in Bernard Levin, *The Way We Live Now* (Sceptre, 1984), pp. 89-92.

2. Derek Kidner, *The Message of Ecclesiastes* (IVP, 1976), p. 89.

3. R. Davidson, *Ecclesiastes and the Song of Solomon (Daily Study Bible*, Saint Andrew Press, 1986), p. 71.

4. See Kenneth Aitkin, *Proverbs (Daily Study Bible*, Saint Andrew Press, 1986), pp. 234-239, and Derek Kidner, *Proverbs (Tyndale Old Testament Commentaries,* (IVP, 1964), pp. 46-49.

5. Jonathan Lynn and Antony Jay (eds.), *Yes Prime Minister: The Diaries of the Right Hon. James Hacker*, vol. 1 (BBC Publications, 1986), p. 128.

6. Robin Corbett and Val Hudson (eds.), *Can I Count on Your Support?* (Stanley Paul, 1986), p. 106.

7. See Aitken, pp. 116-121, and Kidner, *Proverbs*, pp. 42-43.

8. by Stephen Pile (Futura, 1980).

11

CELEBRATING LIFE
11:1-10

Cast your bread upon the waters,
   for after many days you will find it again.
[2]Give portions to seven, yes to eight,
   for you do not know what disaster may come upon the land.

[3]If clouds are full of water,
   they pour rain upon the earth.
Whether a tree falls to the south or to the north,
   in the place where it falls, there will it lie.
[4]Whoever watches the wind will not plant;
   whoever looks at the clouds will not reap.

[5]As you do not know the path of the wind,
   or how the body is formed in a mother's womb,
so you cannot understand the work of God,
   the Maker of all things.

[6]Sow your seed in the morning,
   and at evening let not your hands be idle,
for you do not know which will succeed,
   whether this or that,
   or whether both will do equally well.

[7]Light is sweet,
   and it pleases the eyes to see the sun.
[8]However many years a man may live,
   let him enjoy them all.
But let him remember the days of darkness,
   for they will be many.
   Everything to come is meaningless.

[9]Be happy, young man, while you are young,
   and let your heart give you joy in the days of your youth.

176

Follow the ways of your heart
    and whatever your eyes see,
but know that for all these things
    God will bring you to judgment.
[10]So then, banish anxiety from your heart
    and cast off the troubles of your body,
    for youth and vigour are meaningless.

Maybe this chapter should be prefaced by a government health warning. 'If you are of nervous disposition, you may react badly to what follows. Be warned.'

Your nerves may arise from one of two sources. You may have faced genuine problems in life which have taught you to be very cautious. Alternatively, your spiritual development may have taken place in a strict, puritanical context and you have an in-bred fear of stepping out of line! If either of these is true, you might find the message of the Preacher in his eleventh chapter disturbing and unsettling.

Even if you suffer from neither of these limitations, you may still react badly to what the Preacher is about to say. That is because the atmosphere of our contemporary society is soured by problem-centred thinking. Everyone is expected to have problems, and if you think you haven't any then you really have a huge problem – it's just that you don't know it.

It comes at us all ways. The news media are dominated by the reporting of failure and inadequacy. Minority groups, of all descriptions, are regularly given space to voice their discontentments and to ask for greater help and recognition. Legislation in Parliament is carefully crafted to minimize problems, whether it be in licensing abortion, making divorce easier, or outlawing the eating of meat because of the very slight risk of CJD. It is not usually thought possible to use legislation to uphold central, problem-free, moral truth which a majority accept, but only ever to reduce problems. Social and welfare services, the Health Service and legions of other agencies are all concerned to deal with problems.

I wonder whether doctors ever feel driven to despair at the seeming absence of healthy people in the world. After all, the vast majority of the people they see are unhealthy. A consultant friend was conducting an oral examination in paediatrics one day and completely threw his candidates by asking them to describe what was normal about the child in front of them. They were so used to dealing with abnormalities and had all read up on handling those. But they had lost sight of the normal and healthy. The danger must be that doctors end up thinking negatively.

One of the spin-offs of our present-day climate is that we are becoming an insecure and introverted people – dominated in our thinking by our own problems rather than by our opportunities. Many are paralysed by the problems they face and are completely incapable of taking any steps to overcome them. Instead, they look to other people, not only because they want to blame someone else for their situation, but because they hope that someone else will wave the magic wand and make the problems disappear. When things go wrong the first cry is, 'What's the government going to do about it?' It's never, 'What am I going to do about it?' And if the government does step in and do something, that unfortunately tends to lead to yet more problems. We suffer from such a weight of bureaucracy and legislation that the whole country is in danger of suffocating. You almost need a certificate giving you permission to breathe these days! And that is the result of being problem-centred in our thinking.

The Preacher certainly cannot be accused of being blind to the problems of life. He has not short-changed us as he has introduced us to reality. His long discourse has carefully – some would even say tediously – played the negative music of life over and over again. Listening to him one wonders why he doesn't stay in bed and refuse to get up. He might be forgiven for burying his head in the pillow and refusing to stir once the alarm goes off. It would be perfectly rational to give up on life. But he doesn't. Cynicism and despair could so easily take over. But he doesn't let them.

He has a radical suggestion to make. Instead of dossing around, moping about the problems, he says, 'Celebrate life!', 'Live now!'

His advice as to how you might do that can be grouped under five commands. The choice is yours.

Be vigorous (11:1-2, 6)

Seize the opportunities (11:1)

'Cast your bread upon the waters, for after many days you will find it again.' That curious piece of advice suggests that we should often throw caution to the wind. We may not always be able to calculate the return on our actions; we may not know when our investments will, or even *if* they will, give us a return, but we need to invest in any case. We'll never make a profit unless we take the risk. Let's not hug our resources, our gifts, our opportunities protectively to ourselves for fear that we might lose them. It's only when we are open-handed that we have the possibility of making anything of them which will enrich us and benefit others in the process.

Push the boat out from the shore! Launch out!

Remember the parable Jesus told about the master who went away, leaving his servants money to use in his absence? The one servant of whom he was severely critical on his return was the one who had buried the treasure for fear of losing it. Those the master commended were those who had been adventurous (Matt. 25:14-30).

God has a unique way of causing us to find the bread which

we have scattered on the waters again. Often it returns only after a long time. But it does come back. My wife and I can point to so many times in our lives when this verse has proved true. We have spoken to people about Jesus, or helped them with problems, and seen no positive response from them – until years later, when their spiritual lives have taken off. We have both done courses, and having completed them we have wondered why. They did not seem of any value at the time. But then, sometimes years later, God has picked up just that aspect of our education and given us further opportunities which otherwise would not have come our way. God has a unique way of picking up the loose threads of our lives and weaving them into a beautiful tapestry. We would say we know the Preacher's advice is worth following.

Contrary to the Preacher's advice, many churches exude a spirit of caution that completely contradicts the Preacher's words. They are so respectable, so afraid of giving offence, so fearful that they may step outside of God's will, that they are imprisoned and bound. But *they* have built the prison walls, *they* have locked the door and thrown away the key. God calls them to adventure.

Charles Swindoll brings the Preacher's advice right up to date. He says, 'Don't put your bread in the deep freeze – it'll dry out. Don't store it up in the pantry or seal it in the baggie – it'll mould. Don't hoard it, thinking that it needs protecting – release it.'[1] Years ago Jesus hit at the same calculating caution in the spiritual realm, when he warned, 'The man who loves his life will lose it, while the man who hates his life in this world will keep it for eternal life' (John 12:25).

Seize the many opportunities (11:2)
'Be vigorous' also means that not only are we to seize our opportunities but we are to recognize that they are widespread. Verse 2 is a graphic way of saying that we are to live life in

all its breadth and fullness. The investments we make in life are to be spread around because we do not know which ones are going to fail us, as some are sure to do. 'Seven' and 'eight', the numbers the Preacher refers to, are indefinite numbers. We would speak today about getting involved 'to the nth degree'.

So, don't be boring. Don't rely on one track; that might easily turn into a rut and get you stuck. Life is too rich and varied for you to be narrow.

Unless you are enthusiastic about the multitude of opportunities you face, you may find that the one in which you have invested your time and money is superseded one day by something else. You may no longer find friends who will share your passion for the phonograph, or the steam train, or whatever. You may no longer get the magazines which tell you about it, or the spare parts to maintain it. It may turn sour on you.

And what happens when you come to retirement? Some people live wholly for work, having no other interests at all. Then when the magic age of retirement comes, life suddenly loses all its significance. They have nothing else to live for. And many don't live. They vegetate and die very quickly.

So seize with enthusiasm all the opportunities that God gives you. He is a generous Creator who has given us much to enjoy.

Seize the continuing opportunities (11:6)

You know those two old men who sit up in the box and pass comments during *The Muppet Show*? One can just imagine them commenting on what the Preacher has said. 'Good advice for the young – let's see what they make of it! Ho! Ho!', they'd say with a knowing air. But the Preacher is convinced that this is a message with no age limit attached. We are to seize the opportunities continuously, throughout life, from morning until evening.

After all, the Preacher says, you never know when you will make the breakthrough, which of your projects will succeed, or when.

At different times, God gives you different opportunities. Equally, different things are appropriate at different ages. But at each stage of life, whether you are at morning, noon or evening, seize the opportunities which God gives.

Be enterprising. Launch out in a new direction, knowing that God has created life to be continuously full of opportunities. So maybe, at forty, it's the time to start hang-gliding, and at fifty abseiling, and at sixty wind-surfing! Old age is partly in the mind. You're told you're old and so you start conforming to people's expectations. But there is no need to do so. At every age you can celebrate life.

Be bold (11:3-5)

The Preacher's carefree approach is not a very popular one among some Christians. They would teach us to fear the stance he adopts, for it may lead us into sin. They worry that his advice will cause us to break the rules and transgress. So we restrict ourselves and become terribly inhibited. We bind ourselves with rules, regulations and traditions which prevent us from obeying God's command to enjoy his world.

Our Christian experience is just like an experience Gulliver had on his travels. Having been clobbered by the little Lilliputians, he wrote:

> I attempted to rise but wasn't able to stir, for as I happened to lie on my back I found my arms and legs were strongly fastened on each side of the ground. I likewise felt several slender ligatures across my body from my arm pits to my thighs. I felt something alive moving on my left leg which I perceived to be a human creature not six inches high with a bow and arrow in his hand.[2]

Many of us feel tied to the ground with little creatures crawling all over us, shooting bows and arrows and causing pain to tender and over-sensitive consciences. We need to hear what the Preacher has to say. God our Creator intended us to enjoy his marvellous world, and Christ our Saviour can take us into even greater dimensions of life. So be adventurous. Explore his creation. Enjoy his manifold works and rejoice in his rich gifts.

Some of the chains which tie us firmly to the ground are all too human. We are frail, uncertain and diffident human beings, fearful that we are not in control of our world. So we don't want to do anything which will further jeopardize our security. We don't want to stick our necks out in case our heads get chopped off. It is to those things that the Preacher turns his attention in an attempt to give us greater courage.

Don't be paralysed by inevitability (11:3)

With two brief brush-strokes, the Preacher conjures up a picture of inevitability. If the clouds are full of water it will rain! Where a tree falls, it will lie! It can't help itself. It has no power to move. Both of these events you can anticipate. They are events which are bound to follow.

Even so, life must go on. Don't stay inside just because it's going to rain. Don't miss out on the adventure. Life must go on regardless.

Don't be paralysed by speculation (11:4)

The next picture he conjures up is the other side of the coin. He speaks of the sort of situation in which you don't know what is going to happen. The farmer who constantly looks out and hopes that the weather will be more suitable another day, either for his sowing or his reaping, is not likely ever to do his planting or his harvesting.

How many people have feared to hang out their washing

because they speculated that it would rain and that just as it was drying it would be soaked again? Many of us have missed the opportunity of a lovely drying day because of our forecasting. How many of us use the same excuse to delay doing the gardening (perhaps, however, with more ulterior motives than we would care to admit!)?

Our diffidence often causes us to miss the opportunity. Don't procrastinate. Don't delay but seize the opportunities with both hands, now. As Paul put it, we should be 'making the most of every opportunity, because the days are evil' (Eph. 5:16).

Don't be paralysed by ignorance (11:5)
There are some mysteries we shall never fathom, but we must be careful not to let these prevent us from getting on with life. Science may have helped us to understand much more about the path of the wind and the formation of a foetus in the mother's womb than when Ecclesiastes was written. The illustrations may have to change, but the point remains the same. Not all mysteries can be ironed out here and now. But we shouldn't let that stop us living! We know enough to get on with.

On her 103rd birthday the delightful Salvation Army veteran, Catherine Bramwell-Booth, made precisely that point to a BBC radio interviewer. As if she had lifted her words straight from these verses of the Preacher, she said, 'There are mysteries that we will never know the answer to, but even so you can enjoy life.' If ever a woman had experienced first hand some of life's mysteries she had. But if ever a woman had enjoyed life to the full, she had done that too.

These days a different implication of this verse also needs drawing out. Lord Coggan once commented that with the growth of specialization we are in danger of 'knowing more and more about less and less until soon we will know everything about nothing'! Scientific and other academic research has become so specialized that communication between disciplines is now a major problem. We are also more and more aware of what we do not know and of the way in which any statement we make needs to be qualified before it can be said to be true. Sociologists of language speak of 'seminar language', that is, diffident language which constantly resorts to 'ifs' and 'buts' and 'maybes' and 'on the one hand' and 'on the other hand'. It is not language that can ever commit itself to anything. It certainly finds it hard to make statements of belief or of firm faith.

The bliss of ignorance is that it does not prevent us from getting on and enjoying life in case we are walking into danger! But the Preacher's point is a bit more comforting than that. His final phrase about our ignorance reminds us that God is 'the Maker of all things'. If our attention is directed to him rather than to our knowledge, or lack of it, the situation looks very different. He is capable of controlling things even when we are ignorant about them. He is gracious enough to let us know as much as we need to know. He is the sovereign Lord over all. As 'Maker' his character is to give life, not to ruin it. As Creator he brings life out of nothing and beauty out of chaos. So why be petrified by our ignorance? It would matter only if you were running the universe – and you're not.

So be bold. Do not be paralysed by inevitability, or speculation, or ignorance. Enjoy life.

Be happy (11:7-10)

In three different ways the same message is stated. However many years you live, enjoy them all (verse 8). Be happy while you are young (verse 9). Banish anxieties and cast off troubles (verse 10). The Bible not only permits happiness, it commands it.

Rarely is happiness associated with the Christian faith.

Robert Louis Stephenson once wrote in his diary, 'I have been to church today and am not depressed.' Obviously it was a matter of surprise! He seemed to assume an automatic connection between the two. Since the liturgy stressed that we were all 'miserable sinners', it is not hard to understand why he should do so. Whoever said, 'I might believe in God more if Christians looked a bit more redeemed', had a point.

Of all people, the person who believes in God as Creator and Saviour should be happy. His happiness will not be superficial or glib. It will arise from a profound trust in the living God. He won't slap people on the back when they are facing major problems or enormous pressure or bereavement and shout 'Hallelujah, brother!' or 'Praise the Lord anyway, sister!' 'Reckless words pierce like a sword, but the tongue of the wise brings healing' (Prov. 12:18). None the less, even in pain, there will be that serenity which gives rise to joy. How can such happiness be cultivated?

You can be happy by learning contentment (11:7)
Whatever he may have felt earlier about it being better to be dead than alive, he knows that the truth is different. It really is better to be alive and to experience the light of the day and the glow of the sun. There is always something to be thankful for. Perhaps we moan so much because we take the good things in life for granted – we just assume that we should have them. To stop and think how wonderful they are might reorient our whole approach to life.

Now that he has taken stock, the Preacher realizes that life really is like honey. It is sweet, enjoyable and rich, and we need to savour every mouthful of it with enthusiasm.

Those who have faced some major deprivation in life and then have life restored more fully usually berate the rest of us for taking so many things for granted. The person who can walk again after major heart surgery will tell us how thankful we should be for our health and how careful we should be with our bodies. The blind person who has his sight restored will tell us just how much of the beauty of the world we miss. Sheila Hocken was blind for many years. But then,

> In September 1975 I saw a dazzling unbelievable world for the first time with all its beauty and in all its incandescent colour. For me it was creation itself.... Today has been like no other day since creation, too much, almost, for one human being. Emma [her guide dog] not chocolate coloured but a hundred different shades of brown.... Then there had been the dazzling greenness that I could not make out – grass ... bright beyond belief, just as the entire world had become a landscape, suddenly cleaned like an oil painting, and restored from beneath layers of thick dead varnish.[3]

Everything we need to make us content is ready to hand. We need to open our eyes to see it.

You can be happy by learning carefreeness (11:10)
There are several ways in which anxiety can be banished. It can be done by being irresponsible. It can be done by escapism. But the invitation of the Preacher is to neither of these. His prescription for getting rid of anxiety and off-loading your troubles is an invitation to cast all your anxiety on God, 'because he cares for you' (1 Pet. 5:7).

Surprisingly this advice is directed to young people. I say 'surprisingly' because we usually assume that the young are carefree. But quite apart from the fact that some individuals seem to have been born old and to have missed out on youthfulness altogether, there is increasing evidence of worry and anxiety among the young. Their suicide rate is high. Fears of nuclear warfare, of anxiety about the stability of family life and of their appearance are not far below the surface for a majority of young people these days.

Some older people, especially in the church, need to let

young people enjoy their youth without loading their adult neuroses on them too quickly. Let's give them the opportunity to grow up before we squash them into the adult mould!

But whatever the age, life will be much happier as we learn how to deal with anxiety. Carefreeness is not carelessness. This is not a call to be indifferent about problems or irresponsible about life. Rather it is a call to handle these issues positively. The believer can be carefree as he takes each burden and anxiety to God, knowing that as our loving Creator he's got everything under his control.

As Proverbs says, 'A cheerful heart is good medicine' (17:22).

Be realistic (11:8-9)

Some will misinterpret the Preacher's advice. It sounds as if he has just given permission for people to become posers and flirts, having a good time regardless. Surely he has just encouraged irresponsibility – no matter whom it hurts. But that's not so. He injects just enough realism in the chapter to prevent that. He still has his feet firmly on the ground.

The other side of life provides us with sufficient discipline to prevent us from going overboard. In verse 8 he reminds us that dark days, days of suffering and bereavement, are bound to come. In the same verse, and again in verse 10, he speaks of the omnipresent fact of meaninglessness. In verse 9 he alludes to the restraint that God's future judgment will impose on our lives. That's enough to keep us in our places! As Charles Swindoll says, 'God inserts just enough warning to keep us obedient.'[4]

He is not advocating irresponsibility. He is affirming that in spite of all these mysteries and problems we can still enjoy life. It's what we make of it. By all means let's be responsible and realistic – but let's still be happy.

His note of realism serves another purpose. It debunks

many of the ways in which people commonly think they can find enjoyment in life. Drugs, illicit sex, alcohol, seem to bring enjoyment. Perhaps in the immediate short-term they genuinely do. But then dark days come and they are of no value. Meaninglessness continues unsolved. God's judgment comes and you realize that the destructive power of these apparent happiness-makers has followed you beyond this life. The realism of the Preacher is a strong incentive for finding enjoyment in the more wholesome directions which the Bible recommends.

Realism is not intent on diminishing your joy. But it is intent on taking the hollowness out of it so that you might experience lasting joy.

Be godly (11:5, 9)

The final ingredient for an enjoyable life is God himself. Life can never be truly enjoyed apart from him. We are simply not made to do so. Two aspects of the work of God are mentioned, as a preface to the further development of the theme in the final chapter.

Remember God's care (11:5)

His control of the wind and his miraculous formation of a baby in the womb point to his amazing love and care. Commit all your troubles to him, as verse 10 bluntly commands, and you will find that the strain, stress and anxiety of your life is taken away.

Remember God's judgment (11:9)

From the positive the Preacher moves to the negative. The judgment will keep you in line, not so that you will miss out on things which are good for you, but so that you can enjoy life to the full.

Think for a moment about driving a car. It may seem much

more fun to ignore the pettifogging regulations that warn you to drive on the correct side of the road and stop at red traffic lights. Some do ignore them in the pursuit of fun and adventure. But many who have done so have very soon discovered why those regulations are there. It's no fun to be involved in a head-on smash in which someone is killed because you were on the wrong side of the road. It's no fun to knock an old lady over because you wouldn't stop at the traffic lights. Disobedience to such commands destroys life. It does not enhance enjoyment in life.

So it is with God. We may inwardly protest that his commandments are restrictive and kill-joy. But they are not. He is our wise Creator and really does know best. It's worth following the Maker's instructions. We are likely to get much more use out of the product if we do.

Jesus said, 'I have come that they may have life, and have it to the full' (John 10:10). His disciples ought to be the ones who savour life the most, who drink it in more deeply than others and who enjoy creation to a greater degree than those who do not know its Maker. Because of their relationship with God they should find a dimension of enjoyment that eludes others. The rewards of life should remain untarnished in spite of all the negative experiences they go through. How sad when Christians know little of this.

God encourages us to celebrate life. Let's celebrate it to the full with Jesus Christ who gives life of such a rich quality that the only adequate way to describe it is to call it eternal life.

References
1. Charles R. Swindoll, *Living on the Ragged Edge* (Word, 1986), p.317.
2. Jonathan Swift, *Gulliver's Travels* (Penguin, 1986 edn.), p.55.
3. Sheila Hocken, *Emma VIP* (Victor Gollanz, 1980), pp.1-2.
4. Swindoll, p.337.

12

THE WHOLE DUTY OF MAN
12:1-14

[1]Remember your Creator
in the days of your youth,
before the days of trouble come
and the years approach when you will say,
"I find no pleasure in them" –
[2]before the sun and the light
and the moon and the stars grow dark,
and the clouds return after the rain;
[3]when the keepers of the house tremble,
and the strong men stoop,
when the grinders cease because they are few,
and those looking through the windows grow dim;
[4]when the doors to the street are closed
and the sound of grinding fades;
when men rise up at the sound of birds,
but all their songs grow faint;
[5]when men are afraid of heights
and of dangers in the streets;
when the almond tree blossoms
and the grasshopper drags himself along
and desire no longer is stirred.
Then man goes to his eternal home
and mourners go about the streets.

[6]Remember him – before the silver cord is severed,
or the golden bowl is broken;
before the pitcher is shattered at the spring,
or the wheel broken at the well,
[7]and the dust returns to the ground it came from,
and the spirit returns to God who gave it.

[8]"Meaningless! Meaningless!" says the Teacher.
"Everything is meaningless!"

[9]Not only was the Teacher wise, but also he imparted knowledge to the people. He pondered and searched out and set in order many proverbs. [10]The Teacher searched to find just the right words, and what he wrote was upright and true.

[11]The words of the wise are like goads, their collected sayings like firmly embedded nails – given by one Shepherd. [12]Be warned, my son, of anything in addition to them.

Of making many books there is no end, and much study wearies the body.

[13]Now all has been heard;
    here is the conclusion of the matter:
Fear God and keep his commandments,
    for this is the whole duty of man.
[14]For God will bring every deed into judgment,
    including every hidden thing,
    whether it is good or evil.

Those who have followed the journey so far have travelled a long way. No doubt they have not always liked what they have seen. Far from life being a continuous journey through the Swiss Alps, the English Lakes, or the Canadian Rockies, life is presented as if it were more akin to a journey through the barrenness of the Gobi Desert.

Right to the end Ecclesiastes is haunted by the thought that life is meaningless. There is plenty of evidence to suggest it is. A TV play showed a lad learning bricklaying. He was persistently late for the course, and eventually his instructor blew up. 'You'll never get a job unless you show more responsibility! You've got to learn a trade if you don't want to be unemployed for the rest of your life. And be here on time or no employer will want you!'

The lad threw it all back in his instructor's face. 'What's the point? My dad's a bricklayer and he's been unemployed for nine months!' In a society like ours there is good cause for thinking that life is meaningless.

All our high-flown ideas about life coming crashing down as one futile experience succeeds another. And if they are not all demolished earlier, the final broken bits of meaning are ground to dust in the face of death. That is the greatest meaninglessness-carrier of all. Perhaps, having fully entered into the pain of meaninglessness, we are now ready to accept interpretations of life other than the horizontal interpretations we commonly accept.

Some would argue that any route out of such negativism is just escapism. Marx, for example, who offered his own solutions, suggested that people were bound by real chains of alienation. The trouble was that they covered them up with imaginary flowers to hide the awful reality from themselves. Those pretty flowers, Marx argued, needed to be plucked away so that the true horror of the situation could be revealed. Then people would rise up in revolt and overcome their dependence and at last be free. The plastic flowers to which he referred included religion, and the dependence which he mentioned was a dependence on God, who according to him, did not exist.[1]

The Preacher could not more fundamentally disagree with Marx. He offers a radically different solution. For him there is only one way to cope with reality, and that is not by dismissing God but by acknowledging him. The problem is not that people take God too seriously but that they do not take him seriously enough. The root of the problem is that they are living life 'under the sun', whereas they need to take into account what is *above* the sun as well. Reject God and there is every reason for despair.

The rest of the Bible develops the same message and applies it more specifically to various areas of life. Take the bottom line of death once more as an illustration. It gives us every reason to despair unless Jesus Christ rose from the dead.

But if he really did rise from the dead, and if he did so as a prototype for his disciples, then death is not the cause for despair that it appears to be. With Paul we can sing, '"Death has been swallowed up in victory." "Where, O death, is your victory? Where, O death, is your sting?"' (1 Cor. 15:54-55).

The Preacher's answer to meaninglessness is deceptively simple. It is 'Remember your Creator'. This is the key that unlocks a whole world denied to the unbeliever. Its implications go on being unpacked for the whole of life. But this is the simple starting-point.

Having made the simple pronouncement, the Preacher expands on it a little by telling us *when* and *how* and *why* we are to remember our Creator.

When? (12:1-8)
'In the days of your youth.'

There is an urgency about remembering your Creator. Youthfulness, traditionally, may be a time of carefreeness when the serious stuff of life can be postponed. Tomorrow will do to accept life's burdens and will be soon enough to take on its responsibilities. But life is very brief. If opportunities are not seized now they will be missed. If godly habits are not adopted now it may well be too late. A humorous postcard, seen in a shop recently, brought the message home. 'The best years of life have gone while I was waiting for them to begin.' To drive his message home, the Preacher describes the experiences of old age and death that take hold of us all, stealthily and all too soon.

Before old age (12:1-5)
It may be a little too close to home for comfort, but these verses provide a vivid description of old age. Of course, the commentators disagree about the finer points of interpretation. Some say that these verses are sheer poetry and should

not be applied point by point in a prosaic way.[2] Despite that, it seems the Preacher is saying something like this.

Old age yields little pleasure. It is empty and full of trouble. The body, if not the mind, forces you to become dependent on others once more, and that is a very humbling experience. Many an aged saint has patiently cried to be taken home. Many an unbeliever has resentfully protested about the pointlessness of it all and been anxious to leave it all behind.

Verse 2 says something about the attitude of old age. The sun and light, which are symbols of joy, recede into the background while the storms take centre stage. No sooner has one storm passed than another comes along. There is always some new cause of anxiety or upset.

Verse 3 concerns the body. The 'keepers of the house' are probably the arms and the 'strong men' are the legs. Neither of these are as firm and muscular as once they were. The arms tremble and we become weak on our pins. We are left with few teeth, what he calls 'grinders' (few, at least of our own!). And the eyes begin to fail as the cataracts develop or other defects become more problematical.

Verse 4 speaks of our enforced lack of activity. We become shut-ins; 'the doors to the streets are closed'. Familiar activity like grinding corn is no longer undertaken and seems only a dim and distant memory. But even sleep is denied the old person. There isn't the need for as much as once there was, so the elderly are awake with the dawn chorus. The irony is that they can't hear that chorus because their hearing is going. They suffer a cruel double denial, sleeplessness and deafness.

Four different characteristics are mentioned in verse 5, all typical of old age. The first is fear, of heights and journeys. The second, spoken of by way of a suggestive but less than obvious picture, is of silver hair. When the almond tree blossoms it looks like a distinguished head of silver hair! The third is the difficulty of walking. Sticks and walking frames come into the picture. The fourth is the decline of the sexual drive.

All these are sure signs that death is not so very far away.

Reading these verses recalls that beautiful film *On Golden Pond*. Henry Fonda plays the part of a lovable, foolish old man, full of regrets but unable to express them, touchy and sensitive. His daughter, played by his real daughter Jane Fonda, brings all the bruises of the past to the surface and highlights the limitations of the present. In moving scenes and amid the most beautiful scenery they break through the awkwardness of their relationships and are at last reconciled. Old age then becomes contented and peaceful, but still full of frailties. Many are only too aware of the frailties and never know the joy of reconciliation.

Before death (12:6-8)
Old age may creep up on us, although it usually arrives sooner than we think. Death may creep up on us too, but it may also come all unexpected like a sudden storm. We may imagine we have time to get right with our Creator before old age comes. But we have no certainty at all that we shall reach old age, and so we've no assurance that we shall be able to get right with him before death comes. That's why we need to get right with him as soon as possible – in the days of our youth.

All sorts of imaginative suggestions have been made about the broken cords and shattered pitchers in verses 6-8. Some think he is speaking of a stroke, others of some mystical, out-of-the-body experience. It seems rather that he is simply, if suggestively, capturing the suddenness and violence of death.

He takes up two common pictures from his everyday world to describe death. It is like a silver chain that breaks, irreparably damaging and shattering the golden bowl it was holding up. It is like a pulley that breaks, causing the pitcher it is holding above the well to go crashing down to the bottom and be smashed. It is irrecoverable.

Death may come suddenly. But even if it doesn't, its effects are just as dramatic. Life is finished, irreparable and irrecoverable. Once death does its work, that's it.

He also remarks that death is a cruel reversal of God's intentions. God formed man from the dust of the ground (Gen. 2:7), and gave him life, personality, intellect, capabilities, moral responsibility, and powers of creativity. Death reverses the process and turns us all into dust again, colourless and lifeless. Einstein, Churchill, Mandela, you and me, whoever, all go exactly the same way. No wonder he protests against its meaninglessness once more.

The Christian hope of resurrection puts all this in a different light. Even so, it does not alter the Preacher's argument here. Since death, if not old age, is bound to be our experience eventually, we need to get the most out of life now. And that we will do only if we put our lives at the disposal of our Creator.

Death is a great incentive to belief. To a lesser extent, so is old age. Many in the hospice, or the wards of the hospital where they are spending their final days, review their lives and desire to put matters right, not just with their families but also with God. The Preacher wishes to exploit that fact. It's going to come to us all, so why wait until it does before you know the joy that it can bring if it brings you into a relationship with God? Think what you will have missed because you delayed! Remember that you can never be sure that you will have the chance of getting to know God if you plan a death-bed conversion. Your death-bed arrangements are not within your control.

David Sheppard once remarked that most people think of the church as a kindly body which has nothing serious to say to adults unless they are in trouble.[3] It is for young children and old ladies. It often gives that impression. But how foolish it is to do so. The Preacher knows that nothing could be further from the truth. It claims people in the prime of life and tells them to put their lives into the hands of God. For that is the only way in which life will make any sense at all and the only channel through which any real fulfilment will come.

How? (12:9-12)

These verses are the start of the conclusion of the book. But at the same time they tell us a little more fully what it means to 'remember your Creator'. The command does not mean that we are to think of God occasionally as we might remember a birthday or the Second World War or Sunderland's victory in the FA Cup. When the Preacher uses the word 'remember', he is asking us to do something far more fundamental. He is asking us to make our Creator the foundation of our lives. Everything has to be built and structured on him. We are to stake our lives on our Creator.

How are we to do that in practice? One clear way, if not the only way, is by taking note of what the Bible teaches and obeying it. The emphasis in the final verses is on the words of wisdom which the Preacher hands down to us. We will find that by believing them life will become much more meaningful. And what is true of them is also true of the rest of Scripture.

The Preacher implies that we should do three things about the words of Scripture.

First, *we should acknowledge its truth* (12:9-10). Winston Churchill said, 'Man will occasionally stumble over the truth but most of the time he will pick himself up and continue on.'[4] How true. But if you want to find meaning in life you dare not ignore the truth.

The words of the wise man who stands behind Ecclesiastes are not mere opinion, but 'what he wrote was upright and true'. From what he says here and what we've seen earlier he obviously took time to investigate and be sure before he announced his conclusions. He was also careful to present his findings in as entertaining a way as possible. But the ultimate test is not whether something is entertaining but whether it is true.

There is a danger of forgetting that requirement, even in current Christian circles, let alone in the secular climate. The preachers who are sought after are the ones who can tell funny stories and entertain. Sometimes they may be saying very little or even spouting misleading concepts. Never mind, the saints are entertained and that's what matters. Or is it? The same stricture is even truer when it comes to the news. The choice of stories that make the news, the ways the stories are presented, the order in which they are told, are all governed by their entertainment value. Truth is at a discount in our society and that is dangerous.

If we want to find meaning in life we have got to be concerned for truth, and once we have found it we must acknowledge its authority.

Secondly, *we should accept its correction* (12:11). A shepherd would use a goad (a large pointed stick or a stick with a nail in the end) to keep the sheep going in a direction he wanted. Goads were a stimulus to correct one's path and to alter one's behaviour. Furthermore, when the sheep was poked by one he would tend to remember it.

As Michael Eaton has pointed out, that double-edged effect of the Preacher's words is reflected here.[5] His words are meant to stimulate to action and at the same time to establish his teaching in the memory, 'like firmly embedded nails' (verse 11).

Two things must follow from listening to these words. First, there must be obedience. They are useless unless we put into practice what is said. Secondly, we should base our whole lives on them. They are useless if they have only a short-term effect but then are quickly pushed to the back of our minds. A New Testament wisdom writer, James, makes exactly the same point:

> Do not merely listen to the word, and so deceive yourselves. Do what it says. Anyone who listens to the word but does not do what it says is like a man who looks at his face in a mirror and, after looking at himself, goes away and immediately forgets what he looks like. But the man who looks intently into the perfect law that gives freedom, and continues to do this, not forgetting what he has heard, but doing it – he will be blessed in what he does (1:22-25).

Why should we take any notice of the Preacher's words? Are they not merely the result of his own reflections? Might not some other sage have come up with a different set of ideas? What authority has he got for trying to exercise this correction in our lives and for telling us where we go wrong?

His claim is forthright. We need to pay attention to his goading because his words are 'given by one Shepherd'. The consensus of opinion is that this is a reference, not to an earthly king (although they were called shepherds), but to none other than God himself (Ps. 23:1; 80:1). His words are divinely inspired. Perhaps they are less dramatically inspired than some of the passages of Scripture that carry breath-taking revelations of God's glory and grace. But they are inspired none the less. God has channelled his revelation about life through the mind and pen of a wise man who quietly reflects on his own experience. But since the source of that reflection is God, we must take their message very seriously indeed.

Remembering your Creator therefore involves permitting the Scripture to have a very real effect in changing your life. Attitudes, ambitions, relationships, lifestyle, all need to come under its authority, and a revolution needs to take place. Without such correction, life will remain utterly meaningless.

Third, *we should admit its supremacy* (12:12). The Preacher's next remark has been widely used by bored and wearied students as a cynical comment about their study programmes. But the Preacher is making a serious point.

The burden of his message is, 'Don't go off at tangents and don't get caught up with novelties.' In the field of morality and religion there will always be something new on offer. In actual fact it is probably anything but new, but that is how it will seem.

Since the early 1970s new religious movements have mushroomed. Sociologists may have delighted in describing our world as secular, but the evidence is that, having turned from mainline traditional religions, people have easily accepted a plethora of new religions, some of them obviously absurd. Eastern cults, Transcendental Meditation, Jonestown, Scientology, Children of God, the Moonies, New Age Religion and a variety of other religious novelties seem to hold out answers to the very questions the Preacher has been facing and which traditional churches have failed to address.

The same is true of theories about Jesus. One moment someone has discovered that 'God is an astronaut', the next that he was the founder of a mushroom cult. Theories about Jesus zoom down upon us like reports of the latest marvels of computer technology. If you miss one exciting story, don't worry! There will be another one any minute.

The Preacher warns against going after such novelties. His advice is that you stick to the ancient and tried wisdom. Such novelties appear attractive, but an honest mind examining them will say that not only do they have little going for them, but they are very deceptive in method and quite destructive in result. The evidence for such a conclusion in our own day abounds.

We must sadly confess that the failure of the church to present the traditional Christian message in a forthright and attractive way has often driven people to turn elsewhere. The church is culpable for its failure. But its failure in communication does not mean that its message is wrong and that its opponents' message is thereby established.

Before we are likely to commit ourselves to the teaching of the Bible we must be convinced of its supremacy. If we come to it in a half-hearted way, always looking over our shoulder at some other teaching, then it will not profit us. But once we accept that there and there alone is the truth, it will begin to have a real effect in our lives and bring meaning into the wastelands. There is no room for compromise here. A partial commitment will not profit us. This is, in part, what the New Testament means when it talks about faith. It is the requirement to take the risk of staking your life on the truth of Jesus Christ and him alone. The pick'n'mix approach to religion simply doesn't work when it comes to Christianity. There is no joy or meaning to be found in a little of this and a little of that, in partially trusting in God's Word but hedging your bets by also partially trusting some other teaching.

Something fresh will always be on offer but, the Preacher warns, all that will happen if you chase after it is that you will get very tired. Instead, don't add to the truth of Scripture. Believe it. And you'll find it works.

Why? (12:13-14)

'Now all has been heard....' The Preacher has finished his journey. He has explored the meaninglessness, the boredom, the emptiness and the absurdity of life without God, and has suggested the remedy. To a great extent he has left his readers to pursue the remedy for themselves. Far more attention has been given to the problem than to the answer. Sometimes he has only hinted at the answer, or provided us with obscure clues which should lead us to it. Only in this final chapter has he been explicit, and even then he has been very brief.

The reason for his writing like this is so that the person who has been thinking along with him can be convinced of his own conclusions and not force-fed with the Preacher's conclusions. That does not mean that the Preacher doubts his own answers. In fact, in his final parting shots he gives us two very powerful reasons for 'remembering our Creator'. These two reasons should clinch the argument.

Why you were made (12:13)

In a nutshell, you should remember your Creator because that is why you were created. The emphasis in this verse is on God as Creator and man's relationship to him. If we buy a valuable piece of equipment, we normally find it best to read the maker's instructions and operate the machine accordingly. We can't complain that the washing machine doesn't clean our clothes, if we don't plumb it in, put in the correct amount of soap powder, and let it fill with water. We can't expect it to achieve its aim if we so blatantly disregard what those who made it tell us to do with it. What is more, we don't buy a washing machine if what we want is something to cook fast food. We don't expect a washing machine to function as a microwave.

Yet we human beings constantly disregard our Maker's

instructions and then complain when things don't seem to work properly. We frequently ignore the purpose for which we were made and then wonder why we don't get the results we want. Life would be a lot better if we admitted that our Maker knows what he is talking about, and went along with him.

The command to 'fear God and keep his commandments, for this is the whole duty of man' should not be read as a heavy-duty statement which we have to obey or else. Rather, when the Preacher says it we are to hear him speak with tones which convey the wisdom, the privilege and the joy of doing so. 'Duty' is a word that in recent times has had a bad press. 'Duty' is what we are forced to do when we would rather be doing other things. But not so when it comes to our duty towards God. There is no greater way to meaning and fulfilment and pleasure in life than obeying God. That was the way he made us to tick.

Where we are going (12:14)

The Preacher now faces the other way. Having looked back to our origin he now looks forward to our destiny. Much of it is unknown to us, but there are some things of which we can be sure. One is that we are going to die. A second is that after death comes judgment. A third is that that judgment will be rigorous. So, be prepared. Live now in the light of the coming judgment. The best way to do that is by putting God and his will for you at the very centre of your life now.

You say you don't believe? Well, who is behaving in the most logical way and minimizing the meaninglessness of life the most? The believer or the unbeliever? 'Living under the sun', life without God, makes no sense whatsoever. It's absurd, meaningless, futile, a wisp of vapour. We struggle and puzzle and fight and squirm. But we find no sense or meaning. And in the process we take the huge risk of rejecting what, for good reasons, many firmly hold to be true, that is, the existence of a God who is both our Maker and our Judge, who longs to enrich our lives and give us meaning, but who will one day hold us accountable.

The believer, on the other hand, finds more meaning in life, more sense in its confusing patterns, and more enrichment and joy here, and he is prepared to meet the Judge of all the earth. Even if God does not exist, what has the believer lost? Nothing. What has he gained? Much.

The Christian doesn't easily resort to this form of backs-to-the-wall reductionist argument. He would want to argue that there are many good and positive reasons for believing that the Christian faith is true, not just that it is the safer of two options. But that is about as far as the logic of the Preacher takes him. Without God, life remains a puzzle which makes no sense, and you are driven to the conclusion that a key piece is missing. As you look at life you are forced to conclude that the key piece doesn't exist 'under the sun'. You conclude that the key piece is the eternal God. To posit his existence and to follow his commands makes much more sense of life than anything else.

So, it is wise to 'remember your Creator'. But be careful! To remember him doesn't mean an occasional reference back in your mind to the fact that there is a God. If you are going to 'remember' him it will mean nothing less than staking your whole life on him.

References
1. Karl Marx, *Critique of Hegel's Philosophy of Right*, quoted in David Lyon, *Karl Marx: A Christian Appreciation of his Life and Thought* (Lion, 1979), p.11.
2. R. Davidson, *Ecclesiastes and the Song of Solomon* (*Daily Study Bible*, Saint Andrew Press, 1986), pp. 83f.

3. David Sheppard, *Built as a City* (Hodder & Stoughton, 1974), p.84.
4. Quoted by Charles R. Swindoll, *Living on the Ragged Edge* (Word, 1986), p.365.
5. Michael Eaton, *Ecclesiastes* (Tyndale Old Testament Commentaries, IVP, 1983), p.154.